AN AMERICAN CRIME FIGHTER

AN AMERICAN CRIME FIGHTER

By Lee Richardson, Jr.

Mind-to-Manuscript Publishing

Author: Richardson, Jr. Lee
Cover Designer: Wanda Manning
Editor: Mary Edwards

First U.S. Edition 2017 Soft cover

Richardson, Lee, Jr.
An American Crime Fighter

13 Digit ISBN 978-1-938807-89-3 Soft cover, Perfect Bound

Summary:
This is a memoir written by Officer Lee Richardson, Jr., a 35-year veteran of the Detroit Police Department. Even after retiring his love motivated him to continue police work as a part-time instructor.

Printed in the United States of America

2017 date published

Endorsement

When I was asked to be the editor for this book, I was somewhat reluctant because my genre is Christian literature. However, after careful consideration, I took on the assignment. I am so glad I did. I have served the city of Detroit for over four decades as a community activist and I am almost embarrassed to admit how little I know about the Detroit Police Department. Not only have I served as the editor for this historical book, but I found myself a student. The history contained herein is invaluable. Author Richardson has such a genuine love for the city of Detroit and the Detroit Police Department that I believe he could be an ambassador for both. This is a timely work because all eyes are on Detroit at this time and, without a doubt, Lee Richardson is a true American Crime Fighter with a story that needs to be told and read by Detroiters and others throughout the country.

Dr. Mary Edwards, Editor

Leaves of Gold Consulting, LLC, Detroit

ACKNOWLEDGEMENTS

In addition to my partners that were taken too early, I would like to acknowledge all of the officers that were ambushed, executed, and gave their lives to save others. Included among this acknowledgement are the firefighters who actually run into burning buildings to put out the fires and the fire rescue crew that does all kinds of life-saving acts, such as cutting people out of burning cars, rescuing people from highrise scaffords, etc., and EMS men and woman who also gave their lives.

I'm also grateful to extend this remembrance to all of our military armed forces who gave their lives, served with honor, and continue to do so.

To my children to show that intelligence and love cannot be restrained or stifled by jealousy or hatred.

Just as this legacy cannot nor ever will be destroyed, it is my hope that it will live on through my loyal readers.

TABLE OF CONTENTS

TABLE OF CONTENTS CONT'D

Introduction

My earliest recollection of a Detroit police officer was in the second grade. A Detroit officer visited my school with his trained police dog, a German Shepherd.

After informing my class about the powerful canine police training, the officer called for a volunteer. Just about everyone raised their hands in excitement. Like a dream, I was chosen. The officer instructed me to stand and make a big circle with my tiny arms. No sooner than I made the circle, the large canine came sailing through my arms. The police dog and I were the heroes of the class! I will never forget that day.

I'm now in uncharted waters. Some people I know, or have met briefly, have said, "You should write a book. Your encounters and accomplishments are like an action movie." Well, here goes.

This will not be an autobiography, documentary, or even a commentary, however it is a true story of one police officer's perspective on the discipline and/or make up of what I would like to call, "The Blue Knights in The D."

If there are any names mentioned, aside from my own, they will be changed to protect the innocent and the guilty. I will endeavor to depict for you the most comprehensive logic into the mindset of a Detroit Police Crime Fighter ever written. My goal is to tell a true account through an eye witness (myself) of an urban inner city adventure; to captivate your attention, and satisfy your intellectual appetite for each heart-stopping encounter. These true occurrences will emanate from a world most people are only familiar with through movies, television, the web, or the news media. I will try my utmost to interject you into the midst of true police action. You will feel as though you are right next to my partner and me, in and out of the scout car, in life- threatening situations. Get ready for true life and death action from my first-hand encounters and actual realism that no T.V. writers could ever dream up. This is coming from a city that gets its worldwide bad reputation from a small handful of criminals that seem to get all of the press. Unfortunately, very little light is shed on the majority of good citizens trying to make a difference in a city struggling to shine in an understaffed and underappreciated police force: The Detroit Police Department.

I hope this work might become a suggested or required reading for student police officers in many police academies. The DPD was the first Police Department in the State of Michigan and, in my opinion, the greatest Police Department in these United States. Why? Because we handle more 911 calls than New York City, which has 7 million residents, as compared to around 700,000 Detroit residents since before 2005.

Remember: nothing has changed, or nothing will change, when criminals oppose the law. The criminals want to execute police officers more than we feel the need for the death penalty, although it looks more attractive for every homicide.

Lee Richardson, Jr.

Chapter 1
IN THE BEGINNING

In 1966, I was employed by one of the big three automakers for four years. In my third year, I was approached by management with an offer to become a supervisor. Because I was under 21, they suggested that I take a test for the position. If I passed, they would wait for my 21st birthday to promote me. I passed the exam and was eventually promoted. However, I was told that I must continue to park in the employees' lot and not the executives' lot since the sport car I drove was not manufactured by the company I worked for.

After about a year, I began to notice very large billboards in and around the city of Detroit. The signs depicted a police officer in uniform with the caption that read, "BEING A DETROIT POLICE OFFICER IS MORE THAN JUST A GIG." A month later, I went to the Detroit Police Department Recruiting Office to apply.

On the morning I applied, there were about twenty applicants and a thirty-question test. It was administered by a young police officer in full uniform. He stated that at the end of the exam he would call the names of applicants who scored the highest first. I completed my exam in five or six minutes.

The officer noticed that I was just sitting there. He asked, "What are you doing, cheating?"

Surprised by the allegation, I responded, "No, I have finished!"

Seeming agitated, he said, "You go and sit out front. I will call the names by order of the top scorers first."

I waited out in the lobby, as the other hopefuls finished one by one. The officer came out with a handful of tests. He called my name first, announcing the score of 100%! He appeared shocked and embarrassed when I answered to my name.

Several days later, back at the Recruiting Office, the next phase was investigation of criminal background. I was assigned to an older, tough looking plainclothes officer who already seemed agitated. He asked, "Have you ever been incarcerated?"

I had never heard that term before so I responded with a question, "Do you mean arrested?"

He loudly repeated the question. That's when a uniformed ranking officer appeared from an office door. He walked up to us and asked, "What seems to be the problem here?"

The older officer yelled, "I don't have time to sit here and listen to these lies. This applicant claims he has never been arrested!"

The lieutenant told the officer, "It is not your station to argue with this citizen. He is not an officer yet. Your job is to run his name and other pertinent info thru the L.E.I.N. and N.C.I.C., and wait for the results!"

My name came back stating that I had no prior history or record. At that point, my fingerprints were sent to the F.B.I. with the same results. I felt very proud of my parents' strict upbringing!

The next big test was the Oral Board, which at that time was conducted by three high-ranking seniority officers. I was not aware of their ranks because they were all wearing suits. The Oral Board was a verbal interrogation of your honesty, morals, intestinal fortitude, and quick thinking. I was given a number of police-related situational questions. They liked my answers and straight-forward, aggressive attitude toward wrong doing.

Their last question was, "Why are you not wearing a suit?"

My honest response was, "Because I don't own one."

The three of them busted out with laughter and asked, "When can you start work?"

I responded, "Can I give my employers a two-week notice?"

Still laughing, they said, "Sure, young man, welcome aboard!"

The Detroit Police Academy was located in a civil defense one-story brick building, in a public nature park, with a pond full of wild ducks and birds, and a bridge over the pond.

Every day, at lunchtime, young ladies seemed to appear from nowhere. Recess was great; however, classes were no joke. There was criminal law, state law, misdemeanor, city ordinance, ticket writing, police-related spelling, and report writing. We were told that in a police officer's career he or she will write enough reports to fill an entire library.

In addition to the aforementioned classes, we had physical training, long- distance running, firearms training, firearms class, rifle, shotgun, military weapons, crowd control, teargas. In teargas training, you go thru a chamber full of gas. Some who did not follow instruction became gassed. The rest who listened were sent back through without a mask just for the experience. It was terrifying not being able to breath. More classes: self-defense, physical arrest procedures, radio instruction and, for the first time, our class was to spend three days in the county jail with the Wayne County Police. Afterwards, we were to be tested on all of these categories. It was mandatory that you pass each one of these categories or start over with the next class.

Our class consisted of about 82 student patrolmen and one student patrolwoman. There were two veteran police officers and one sergeant. The two patrolmen were called TAC officers. No relation to TMU. The three of them took turns instructing our class.

The sergeant was the most senior officer and was quite laid back. One Saturday morning he took our class to the airport. That is when we discovered he was a pilot. The sergeant explained to us that this was the beginning of the DPD Aviation Section. There was one single-engine airplane. The city was in the process of purchasing several used helicopters. It was an exciting day and time to be a student in the academy.

Chapter 2
MY FIRST ARREST

On Graduation Day, we anxiously received our assignments. The Viet Nam War was still on and everyone wanted to go to the most dangerous precincts in the city. We were the new breed and looking for action. For the first time, our occupation was considered a profession, since many of us, including myself, had some college background.

About five of my classmates and myself were assigned to a precinct I had never heard of. Little did I know that I would find all of the action that I could handle there. My world was about to change forever!

I learned quickly how protective my parents had been over me and my siblings. I also came to realize that what we had learned in the academy only qualified us to pass the exam, not how to survive. We had no idea that we were only babes in the woods surrounded by blood thirsty wolves!

One salty officer approached us and said, "You guys are like babies. You don't know anything. Now, your real DPD training is about to begin." I had a bad feeling he was right; and he was!

The next day, after roll call, we were just standing around like spare parts, while the sergeant looked for places to fit us in. I was assigned to two tough-guy types who told me to sit in the back seat. (There were no shields in those days). I was told to, "Shut up and don't touch anything!"

I responded "SIR, YES SIR!"

Around noon, the officers called dispatch for lunch. They ordered, "You stay here!" I remained in the cruiser for their entire lunch period and for the rest of the shift. I said to myself, "*I get it. This is another test, another boot camp. If I break, I would either tell on them or quit the force. I will not break.*" It would take a year to be confirmed, which meant that you are not in the union and have no protection from termination. This meant: follow orders and walk on rice paper!

Finally, my first assignment was to the Tactical Mobile Unit (T.M.U.) This unit was born out of the 1967 Riot in Detroit. They drove high visibility scout cars: white in color with two blue overhead rotating lights, one on each side of the roof. After the riot was over, they were assigned from precinct to precinct according to high crime volume, day by day. Their method of operation (M.O.) was to meet up at a given location and travel as one group to the precinct that was backed up with crime. The theory was sound, however, when things were slow they seemed to get underfoot of the regular precinct officers. When the T.M.U. officers left for another assignment, the citizens would be irate toward the regular officers. Not long out of the academy, I was unaware of these concepts. I was assigned to two seasoned officers as a three-man crew.

After about a week of observation, I convinced the crew to stop a vehicle that I thought suspicious. There were four occupants. The three in the front seat were moving around frantically. The vehicle was pulled over and my two senior partners covered me as I requested the occupants to please exit the vehicle.

It was a nippy fall night. For officers' safety, I patted down the male occupants for any weapons. The female occupant was in the center of the front seat. When she exited, she was moving in an odd fashion. I asked her what was wrong. She stated she was cold and needed to go to the restroom. I took her hand and said, "Step away from the vehicle." As I pulled her, a nickel-plated 38 snub-nose revolver she was holding between her thighs fell to the pavement from under her skirt. I told her, "I have a present for you, a bracelet." She held her hands out as I cuffed her and read her rights to her. My partners were very impressed. Later, I received a written accommodation for taking a gun off of the streets.

Chapter 3
THE 13TH PRECINCT

My next and permanent assignment was, let's call it, the 13th Precinct. It was an unassuming looking building and did not even look like a police station. However, it was unlike any other precinct, housing an array of restaurants from greasy spoons and fast food to very expensive high-end dining clubs. We had more choices to eat than any other precinct.

On the midnight shift, scout car crews came from all over the city, because there was always something open. This precinct was also unique unlike any other in the U.S. because of the Students for a Democratic Society, (S.D.S.) The Weathermen and the headquarters of the Black Panthers, all in one precinct! These groups were all dissidents of the status quo and enemies of law enforcement everywhere. Our precinct was the only one in the city where the parking lot was bombed. There was no video surveillance then. To prevent further bombings, scout car crews took turns all over the city at all precinct stations to overlook station security. It consisted of one scout car and a two-man crew to watch the lot for one hour per crew. This type of security went on indefinitely and proved successful.

Almost every business owner gave us a warm welcome. I particularly remember a married couple that owned a bar and grill. The first time I met them they remarked how young I was and asked, "Have you ever had a kielbasa sandwich with Sauerkraut?"

I responded, "No."

"You just wait!" they excitedly said. They fixed my first polish sausage sandwich. From that point on, they treated me like a son and made me promise to come and visit them often. I felt protective over them so I did just that.

I was mainly partnered up with an officer who had only one year on the force. He talked a lot about how we had to watch out for the SDS and the Weathermen. Looking back, I have noticed that only the names have changed; the politics remain the same. Terrorists, militia, separatists, America for the So called Americans, Nazi style skinheads, and numerous other hate groups all dislike the government but they hate the police!

The year 2014 was not a good year for our ranks; the war against police officers took a toll. Sadly, the loss of life suffered by our children at the hands of ruthless cowards is just as devastating.

It is my sincerest wish that as you continue on this literary journey with me that citizens and police officers alike find the knowledge and the wisdom to protect yourselves from harm. I learned early on the force that over 95 % of the citizens are good law-abiding people and 4% are of the criminal element; 1% of those are career criminals. These are the ones who love what they do and have no remorse. Just imagine a lawman's task. In addition to dealing with this horde, you must be a social worker, a psychiatrist, a big brother or sister, a marriage counselor, deliver babies, give first aid, give legal advice, appear in court whenever summoned, be prepared for any violent contingency, and take control of any emergency situation, hazmat (handling hazardous materials), hazardous storms, flood emergencies, barricaded gunman, attempted suicides, hostage situations, bomb threats, explosions, assist firefighters and fire victims, save lives whenever and wherever possible and, most of all, be prepared for ambush to protect your partner and yourself. This will enable you to live to fight crime and save lives another day. To be able to return to duty day after day is an absolute must.

Chapter 4
NOTHING IS "ROUTINE"

Just to show you how some things never change, these next facts are as timely today as when I went through the academy some 45 years ago!

During my police academy days, one of my favorite instructors was an older gentleman, actually a retired inspector. He was now teaching at one of our universities. This learned gentleman illustrated that a police department is likened to a minority community. Therefore, if one police officer commits a crime, or does something terribly wrong, the whole police department gets the blame by most of the public. By the same token, when a member of a minority does the same, it is perceived that all minorities are criminals.

These days, with the internet connection, all of the police departments in the country receive the blame. In retrospect, I must say that the Detroit Police Department's image has improved dramatically since 1998. When it comes to percentages, I would estimate that over 99% of all police officers are honest and try their best to serve and protect. This is coming from my three-and-a-half-decade career perspective.

One afternoon, as I boarded the elevator for Communications on the sixth floor of 1300 Beaubien, a young man and his son got on right after me. The young man said to his son of about five years, "Do you see that policeman? If you are not good, he will grab you and throw you in jail!" The child looked at me in fear. I immediately told the young father, "No, please don't say that! If he ever needed help or was in trouble, he would be afraid go to an officer. He might even illicit help from a drug dealer or child molester. Every child should know that all police officers are their protectors and friend."

The young father looked at me with a mixture of surprise and shame. He quickly apologized, stooped down next to his son, and said "Son, Dad was wrong. Remember, all police officers are your friends!"

We all smiled at each other and I thought to myself, "Made two more friends." It was a good day.

While patrolling in an urban environment, you will encounter citizens who have quite a few problems. Some minor, many are major. This is where I learned that I had many roles to play. Given the authority as a representative of the people and the state, my partner and I dispensed the law as we saw fit for our community. For example, on one police run we encountered a woman who wanted us to spank her son. She said he was unruly and she could not handle him since there was no father in his life. My partner and I quickly decided against the spanking, sat down and gave him some fatherly advice at great length. I would like to think that he is still out there, all grown up, and a credit to society.

On another police run, an elderly woman informed us that a boarder in her home had gone berserk, overturned his bed, and caused a disturbance with the other tenants. I took him outside and graphically depicted to him (with a large black jack that I carried for show and never had to use) what I would do to him if I ever had to come back. We never got another call back there again. This saved him from an arrest and her from having to deal with him upon his release.

No matter how minor, you must understand that almost every caller believes that his or her problem is of the utmost importance. My partners and I treated the public as though their call was most important.

I always instructed new rookies to try and make friends while on patrol, because we have our share of enemies. When you put on a police uniform and expose that uniform to the public, you set off a whole range of emotions: admiration to envy, love to hate, acceptance to rejection, and understanding to violence. For those that respect you, you represent safety and security, a warm feeling! For those that hate you, you represent opposition, oppression, a deterrent to the crimes they would ordinarily commit, if it were not for your presence.

In many ways, we are the culmination of all of the problems, downfalls, rejections, family trouble, joblessness, and downright hatred for the law, authority, and order. Most new officers do not realize this danger. However, take it from me, learn from your senior or retired officers, and learn fast. In this profession, you don't live to retire by being naïve. No matter how quiet your city, township, town, or hamlet, be advised that on this job, there is no such thing as routine. No day or night, no police run, no patrol, no investigation, no disturbance, no barking dog, no noise complaint, and most of all, no traffic stop, or family trouble is routine!

5 Chapter
LISTEN TO THOSE WHO KNOW

On or off duty, I always looked for the good in people I encountered. There were some that I could not reach. In some instances, where a physical threat to me and my partner was eminent, I have pleaded with them not to attack me and put them on notice. This happens quite frequently and I never lose a fist fight.

As you may have guessed, my request usually fell on deaf ears. On one occasion, an assailant awakened in police lock up in the hospital. He asked, "What did that officer hit me with?"

The officer simply answered, "His fist!"

For the prisoners that attacked my partner, I became very relieved when the cuffs went on. As long as the cuffs were on, they were safe from any other officers or citizens. This was my personal guarantee. For as many physically forceful arrests we have made, as well as knock-down drag out fights won, I never received a citizen's complaint, ever!

It was on an overcast summer day when we got a police run for a felonious assault (F.A.) that had just happened. Upon arrival, we talked to two women and an 11-year-old female. They all had head wounds and were covered in blood. The occupant who reported the offense informed us that her brother broke a metal table leg off of her table and beat them with it. She also stated that this was an unprovoked attack and she would be the complainant for the prosecution. She told us that her brother was half a block away at her mother's house. We called for the medics and headed to the mother's house. It was a two-family flat upstairs.

We informed the mother that her daughter, granddaughter, and her daughter's friend were all assaulted by her son. The mom was not happy. When we told her we wanted to talk to him, she pointed him out. He was on the phone. We told him to hang up, because we wanted to talk to him. He swore at us. His mother said, "You don't talk to the police that way!" We moved to make our arrest and he resisted. I overpowered him. The perp ranted and raved down the stairs, all the way to the station, and threatened he would kill me when we took off the cuffs.

Inside the lock up, we told the doorman that he wanted the cuffs off so he could kill me. As the doorman attempted to remove the cuffs, the perp became hysterical, screaming, "No, don't take them off!"

I remarked, "Just as I thought; a woman and child beater will not fight a man!"

Since the beginning of law enforcement in this country, in general, lawmen have been hunters of men. Hunting humans is the most dangerous game. Humans are unpredictable, resourceful, can travel great distances, change their appearance, and can be aided by a relative, friends, or fellow criminals. Any given lawman or woman is faced with an array of blood thirsty criminals: career criminals, serial killers, murderers, serial rapists, arsonists, and those spaced out on mind-altering drugs. There are those invisible ones with no criminal past who suddenly snap and ambush officers, commit suicide for unknown reasons, just to make a statement, or for revenge. The ambush of a defenseless officer has not changed since the Wild West! Being a peace officer is one of the most danger-filled occupations in the world, for there are so many different types that hate us; sometimes even in our own neighborhoods.

As I have mentioned, 2014 was a bad year for law enforcement, insofar as loss of life and several other aspects. However, there is an upside to those dreadful statistics. Stay fit. Your enemies do. Let me repeat. Talk to seasoned officers. There is a world of untapped survival skills waiting for you just for the asking. These are largely free resources that can save you or your partner's life. It was the old-timers' knowledge that saved my life more than once. Keep in mind that most of these senior officers were World War II vets and no one's chumps. The wisdom they imparted to me gave me respect. They took me under their wings and protected me as if they were my parents. My father is also a former WWII vet, and I have been in the habit of listening to my elders for quite some time.

Chapter 6
"OFFICER IN TROUBLE"

It was a very cold and blustery winter night during my first year on the force. My partner and I were up for one hour of station security. As the junior man in the car I got the parking lot, while my partner guarded the warm garage. It was so cold I had to run the engine the entire hour to keep warm.

Just as we were being relieved to patrol, an "officer-in-trouble run" crackled over the mobile radio. "All cars such and such address, an officer in trouble, possible undercover drug bust gone bad, shots fired!"

My partner (with one year on the job) and myself (with only months) were the first to respond. "Radio 13-4 is on the way!!" It had just turned dark as we started on our way to the edge of the precinct.

We arrived at what we thought was close to the scene. I exited the passenger side of the car and ran to the sidewalk in front of a dark house. When I became aware of the fact that we were the only car there, I cautiously took several steps forward. All at once several shots rang out from the house that I was directly in front of.

In an instant, it was clear to me that I was in the line of fire. Fragments of ice and snow hit me in the face and chest from the bullets bouncing off of the sidewalk inches in front of me. I fell back to take cover. Realizing my rookie mistake, I prepared to return fire.

Just as I took aim at the location of the muzzle flashes, I saw movement. I said to myself, "*I can't miss this perp. He's trying to escape*," I took careful aim and noticed a gun in his hand. I couldn't believe my eyes. He was walking straight towards me! In that instant, and in less than a second, all of my training focused on the trigger of my department-issued weapon. With maximum pressure before the hammer raised, I ordered, "Police officer, freeze!"

To my astonishment, he kept coming toward me! Just as I was about to fire, I noticed his gun was pointed straight down and he was holding his gun arm. He had been shot. I asked myself, "Could this be the undercover officer?" As he walked past me looking me in the eyes, a voice said, "Don't make a second rookie mistake!" He never said a word, he just kept on walking. I followed him with my gun sight until I was sure of no further threat.

As I watched him disappear, I turned my attention towards a stream of red and blue lights coming from a distance. There were about 15 scout cars responding to the "officer-in-trouble" call! Upon their arrival, I pointed out the drug house and told them the officer had escaped. In an instant, these experienced officers started surrounding the house. I moved a block away and watched as they began the assault on the drug house. Minutes later they came out with all of the occupants under arrest. There were no further shots fired. I was impressed!

I was still having trouble at roll call getting a partner to work with, so they paired me with the one-year wonder again.

It was a warm spring day; my first on the job. The afternoon shift had just started. We were completing the scout car inspection on the police ramp. Then it came over the air, "Officer-in-trouble such and such location near the university!" This was my second "Officer-in-Trouble" run. We were very close and responded first. "Radio 17-3 is on the way!"

First on the scene, we observed a huge unruly crowd. Without thinking, I told my partner to wait as I jumped out of the car.

I could see over the crowd and spotted a university officer alone and surrounded by a sea of angry party goers. I made my way through the hostile mob, grabbed the officer and his arrest, and walked them both away, untouched by the crowd. It seemed like a mile. I got them in the scout car and yelled to my partner, "Get out of here!" We sped off while the crowd stood there stunned. The officer was a Wayne State University police officer. Their first office was right across the street from my 13th Precinct.

We raced back to the station and took the officer and his prisoner to the lock up and secured the perp in the bull pen. We reported to the lieutenant on the desk. As we were doing so, a crowd busted into the front door and into the precinct lobby. The lieutenant tried to talk to the crowd, as they demanded release of the prisoner. At this point, he saw communicating with the crowd was useless.

We were calling for backup when the lieutenant said, "Arrest them!" The inside officers jumped over the desk. We assisted. Needless to say, there was an enormous brawl. In addition to our cars, scout cars from neighboring precincts were responding. Eventually, we were able to secure the front door and lock up the crowd trapped in the lobby. They were all held for inciting a riot, refusing a police order to cease and desist, and resisting arrest. They were later put through the system. (Checked though L.E.I.N. and N.C.I.C.). Most were released. They had no prior record. It was a good day of police work, as no one was seriously injured.

Unknown to me, word had gotten around the precinct station about the initial "Officer-in–trouble" run. At the next roll call, the senior officers were arguing over who was going to partner with me in their car. On the force, most everything was dictated by seniority. Therefore, I was assigned to the most senior officer on the shift. Things were about to look up for this probationary officer, along with a reputation for aggressive quick thinking action and the preservation of a university officer's personal safety.

The months seemed to pass by quickly and it was confirmation time. I had made it. I was now a full-fledged "Detroit Police Officer," complete with a union membership card and a permanent assignment to my precinct.

One year on the job. What a rush. I had passed all of the obstacles, roadblocks, and tests put before me. My willpower and discipline had prevailed. In those days, you usually walked a beat for several months. However, at my station, they had more scout cars than officers, so straight to the streets I went with pleasure.

7
Chapter
ON MY OWN

In 1970, The Detroit Police Department was over 6,000 strong. During the summer afternoons and midnights, we were kept extremely busy. It was not long before I became second man on my crew, which meant when my senior partner was on leave or furlough, I was senior man. This position came with great responsibility, as well as respect. It also meant that anything that went wrong with the cruiser, or any mistakes my junior partner made, I would be held accountable.

There were quite a few military men returning from the Vietnam War. They were joining the force in large numbers. I was beginning to notice that too many of them were being killed or injured on the job. The only cause I found was that once some of them returned back to the world they became a little too relaxed. On the DPD, there is no such thing as relaxing, on or sometimes off duty. I made it one of my missions to take my protectors of our nation under my wing, as the old timers had done for me.

It was a pleasant summer on dayshift. I was senior man and had a brand new rookie assigned to my car. He was not ordinary. He was a Nam Vet and his first day on the job. I took most of the first hour explaining to him how he was now wearing a different target and how to survive using my urban street tactics, paying attention to every detail and everyone around, especially split-second thinking and decision-making according to training and discipline. This continued and ultimate training is classified.

We left the ramp and started to patrol, heading for our scout car area at prowling speed: a speed at which we could observe the most activity.

All at once we got our first run of the day.

"13-4 meet an officer about a B&E phone booth."

On the way, radio 13-4," I replied!

Upon arriving at the scene, I saw a familiar police officer standing next to a damaged phone booth. He told us it looked as though the perps tried to take the whole phone booth and that there was a suspicious pair that just turned the corner.

I told him, "We will check them out!"

As we turned the corner, we saw the pair about half way down the block. When we pulled up next to them I said, "We want to talk to you!"

One of them broke running back the way we came.

I told my partner, "Cuff the one who froze and wait here for me!"

I backed the scout car up. The fleeing perp turned into the alley. As I sped up the alley he vanished. I knew he had to have turned right. So I ran up the connecting alley. As I came to the end of the alley, I saw a nun standing inside a fence. She was pointing to my left. I saw a parking lot with only one car in the lot and nothing else. Knowing something was not right, I instinctively pulled out my department issued 38 caliber service revolver. As I approached the parked car, I noticed some movement underneath. I ordered "Police officer, come out!"

As the perp stood up, he instantaneously fired two shots point blank from one side of the vehicle. I was standing on the other side. The other round came from his 380 caliber semi-automatic! One buzzed by my right ear. As I returned fire, the second shot zipped by my left ear and I dove behind the scout car. A gunfight ensued! I should have died that day.

I took time to call out my location and info, "Radio, 13-4 is at such and such location, shots fired!"

My heart sank when dispatch responded, "Unit calling, your radio is breaking up, unable to read!"

Realizing I was on my own, I took careful aim at the felon who was watching me through the car window. I fired the accurate round aimed between his eyebrows. To my amazement, the round bounced off of the car's window. Now the felon took off running down the next block over.

I remembered that now would be a good time to call out again my location and for back up. Cautiously, I approached his last location. I could hear the old timers talking to me. The perp is going to lay against the wall of the apartment building with his gun arm stretched out against the wall, waiting for me to follow him around the corner where he would have the advantage of a more perfect kill shot. However, I appeared where he never thought I would be. This time I had the cover of a parked car on the street. My weapon aimed at him but I didn't fire. The felon took off running and I lost sight of him. I radioed his physical description and direction of his escape. As I ran toward his last location, down an alley and inside a fence, a very small girl pointed and said, "Man ran into that house." I radioed dispatch of the address. He was now trapped in a vacant house.

I updated dispatch of the new location. Then I remembered my partner. He had found the scout car with his prisoner, engine still running and thought I had bought it (been killed). I radioed him to meet me at the scene of the abandoned house the perp had broken into.

After I was picked up, we made the scene in front of the vacant house. By this time, the police response was overwhelming; police were everywhere! Three or four officers had trapped the felon under the front porch. They were fearlessly standing and stomping on the porch ordering the perp to come out.

I went to the front of the yard and could see the felon through a brick hole under the porch. He was still armed! I took careful aim again and had a perfect head shot. A senior police officer cautioned me to wait to see if he surrendered.

"Throw out the gun!" the officers on the porch shouted, still disregarding their own safety. The perp was looking me dead in the eyes, as he threw out the weapon.

"Stick your hands out!" they shouted again. As he did, they pulled him through the hole, bricks and all!

"Here's your arrest, officer," they replied as they handed him to me covered in dust.

To tell the truth, I was fuming with anger that I had to take him alive. Moments before, he had tried to ambush me without warning and kill me without remorse. Just then, my discipline and training took over. Everyone was watching, especially the new rookie I had to lead by example.

On the way to the station, I was still wondering why this young criminal wanted to execute me. All I wanted to do was ask him a few questions. I was about to find out why my profession could be so deadly.

We processed the prisoner, took his prints and property, along with multiple 380 rounds found in his pockets. We ran his name and prints through L.E.I.N. and N.C.I.C. and got a hit from both entities on the Green Monster. (An old teletype machine that typed about as fast as I do). The machine was slow; however, it rarely broke down. This time there was something strange. It typed almost half an hour! This turned out to be the longest criminal record on any criminal I had ever arrested. He was wanted for numerous assaults and batteries, (A&B's), several breaking and entries (B&E's) several hold ups, several UDAA's, several gun-related CCW's, and one bank hold up. Finally, he was wanted by the U.S. Military for desertion.

It now became clear to me why he would rather see me dead than be apprehended. He never saw me as a human being. In his mind, all he saw was the uniform and an end to his criminal career, which almost ended in the one thing he had not yet done, commit murder on a police officer.

I was truly disappointed with the performance of my department-issued weapon. The very next payday I went to the last gun shop left in Detroit. It was on the corner of W. Forest and 12th street. I told the shop owner that I needed a more effective weapon than the one I carried. He brought out several weapons; however, none were department approved. He thought for a minute and said, "Wait. I've got one more in the safe."

Becoming impatient I said, "Okay."

He returned shortly with a polished wooden box. He proudly said, "This is the only one in any gun shop in Michigan!" He opened the box and revealed a very large blue steel revolver. I asked, "What's that?"

He proudly replied, "A 44 Magnum. The same type the police detective Dirty Harry carries in the movie!"

I was not familiar with the weapon or the movie, but as I removed the gun from the bed of green velvet, it was love at first sight! It cost almost my whole paycheck, but I did not care. I said, "Write it up!"

Several weeks later I was summoned to criminal court where the trial of my court case had taken place. At the hearing, the defense waived a jury trial.

My testimony as a uniformed police officer in front of a jury, as the victim and the complainant, would be an instant guilty verdict. The defense took a plea bargain for lesser time.

As far as the prisoner's extensive criminal record was concerned, attempted murder of a police officer now topped his lawless career. He received the maximum sentence in a prison where he would not be very popular because the prison guards do not like police shooters.

As far as my new street weapon was concerned, don't get the wrong idea. I was not in the market for a super weapon; I only wanted a weapon that at least could effectively penetrate an auto glass. Later, on the street, and in potentially deadly situations, the 44 turned out to be a life saver. It made those who had violent intentions think twice, and then think again! I can imagine it's no fun looking down the barrel of a deadly 44!

Chapter 8

IN THE PRESENCE OF DEATH AGAIN

It was a warm summer day. My partner and I entered an apartment building on a (routine) investigation.

As we proceeded through the narrow hallway, all at once a woman appeared from an apartment with a large butcher's knife. In an instant, I pulled my weapon. She had my partner trapped against the wall, the knife a foot away from his chest. "I will kill you!" she shouted!

My partner was frozen still. "Miss, drop the knife now!" I ordered. She refused. I told her, "If you make the slightest move in any threatening way, I will shoot!" I had every right to discharge my weapon right then; but heaven knows I did not want to kill this woman. It was obvious she was having an emotionally bad time. I warned her again, "If I have to shoot, you will not survive. It was a standoff, and I did not want to be there in this situation. I'm sure my partner felt the same way, only ten times over!

It seemed like an hour had passed with the three of us like statues standing in the hallway.

My partner and I had completely forgotten about our portable radios. In this situation, they were of no help anyway.

Just then, an older woman came into the hallway from her apartment. She knew the young woman and shouted her name, "What are you doing? They are the police and they will kill you!"

The woman stated, "I don't care. I'm going to kill this one!"

Reluctantly, I pulled back the hammer of the 44 magnum. There were several loud clicks, as the hammer reset for a single action shot.

The woman's neighbor shouted, "Please don't shoot officer!" She said, "Girl, give me the knife or we won't be neighbors anymore; you will be dead!"

The girl's neighbor slowly eased up to her, took the knife, and dropped it to the floor. Then she hugged the woman as if to shield her from me.

"Can I take her home to my apartment?" she pleaded.

I gave approval, "Get her some help!" I slowly released the hammer to neutralize my weapon.

You may be thinking, "What, no arrest?" No, my partner and I were elated that he was alive; and I also was elated that I did not have to take her life. I'm certain the young woman is also glad to be alive.

Just as before in the previous fire fight, after the shift was over I had time to reflect. My hands started to shake! This reminded me of how close I stood in the presence of death again. This one thing seemed to always prevail. The very next day, my gun hand was back steady as a rock. However, I knew this would not be our last encounter. Me and death would meet again.

Chapter 9
INTERNAL AFFAIRS

Sometime around the 1940's, decades before I joined the force, Internal Affairs began to appear. I knew nothing of this section until one day my partner and I received a police run, "Such and such address. A shooting just occurred!"

We responded, "17-3, on the way, radio!"

Upon arrival at the scene, we encountered a male shooting victim outside of the location. He had been shot in the head with a small caliber handgun. The bullet had penetrated his scalp and traveled around his skull to his forehead, coming to rest as a knot over his eyebrow. He stated that a family member had tried to kill him but he escaped by jumping out of the second story window!

We called for a police wagon to transport him to Detroit General Hospital.

Before we could investigate the second floor for the shooter, another scout car showed up and said they would take over the search, while my partner and I secured the lower perimeter.

There was a female occupant in the home who waited on the first floor out of danger. After a few minutes, the other scout car crew brought down a double-barrel shotgun and stated the perp had escaped and the upstairs was clear. They left the scene.

My partner and I questioned the occupant further, left for the station to complete our report, and go off duty.

Early the following morning, I was awakened by a phone call stating the female occupant had made a complaint against my partner and me. We were ordered to IA, on duty and in full uniform.

Upon arrival, we waited in an office about an hour. Then we were approached by two men in plain clothes and told we would have to take a lie detector test. We were not told why. They took us to an office in a commercial building just about a mile north of the city limits located on Greenfield and Nine Mile Road. Once there, we were separated into two separate offices. The lie detector expert introduced himself and told me what questions he would ask. After I was hooked up with a series of wires, he proceeded to ask the questions we had reviewed; however, the last question he asked me was not on the list. It was an unfair trick question. "Have you ever done anything on the job that you could be fired for?"

After all of my honest answers, this one was designed to make me fail. All I could do was answer honestly, "I don't know!"

The machine reacted to my response and he quickly turned it off.

After the unfair lie detector test was over, the two IA officers entered the room. I angrily asked them, "What is this all about?"

The older sergeant came clean and stated they were there because of a complaint that two officers had stolen over $600.00 dollars from an upstairs bedroom dresser drawer. What was devastatingly worse was that the woman had described the two officers that had gone upstairs to the letter and described my partner and me as the two officers that had stayed downstairs. The IA officer had further confessed that they had already suspended the two guilty officers, pending their termination.

With an offensive tone I asked, "Why then did you put my partner and me through this unfair, grueling interrogation?"

They explained, "To catch you in a lie or any other illegal activities, so we could prosecute you as well!"

After learning of this feeble attempted sabotage of two honest officers' careers, I went into a silent rage. Knowing that we were innocent, they went through all of this deception.

On the ride back to our scout car, one of the younger officers had the audacity to ask us, "If you see any officers in your precinct involved in any illegal activity, let us know."

Just then, I lost it! Riding in the back seat of their unmarked car, I told the sergeant just what I thought about their unprofessional, attempted smear tactic. I used such explicit verbal terms that the young driver almost lost control of the car while driving on the freeway. Then I threatened him with great bodily harm if he had an accident. There was no further conversation until we were driven back to our scout car.

CHAPTER NINE - "Internal Affairs."

My senior partner was shaken at my violent verbal reaction to the IA officers and their feeble attempt to recruit us as snitches. I had several more run ins with IA; each one as bad as the next. By this time, they had succeeded in recruiting a formidable enemy: ME, THE CRIMEFIGHTER!!

Chapter 10

BEFORE E.M.S.

Long before there was an E.M.S. the Detroit Police was THE only public emergency ambulance service in Detroit.

In the early 1970's, only two of the big three auto makers still made a station wagon. Every precinct kept two wagons on the street at all times: one in the north and one in the south of all precincts. The wagons played a critical part of emergency service; one wagon for seriously injured police officers and children; the other for citizens. This turned out to be my next assignment. I checked with my sergeant to find out why I was assigned. He told me he had looked at my application and found that one of my hobbies was weight lifting. I reluctantly decided to make the best of it.

There was almost nothing we could refuse to transport. The wagons had four doors and two stretchers side by side on wheels that hooked to locking clamps behind the rear seat. We had very little in the way of medical equipment or training. However, we did have three things in our favor: large block V8 engines, blinding speed, and highway and street race driver experience; another hobby.

We could convey the most critically injured from anywhere in the precinct to Detroit General Hospital (DGH) in two minutes or less, usually less. We conveyed a wide-range of victims: heart attacks, shootings, stabbings, car accidents, felonious assault, burns, suicide attempts, assault and battery, all kinds of drugs: LSD, heroin, cocaine, angel dust, marijuana-laced with embalming fluid, alcohol poisoning, and many more.

We rarely received any standard police runs at all and were kept in reserve as specialized units. However, in the summer and especially on weekends, we conveyed almost non-stop medical runs; otherwise, we were kept in reserve for serious back-up when absolutely needed.

In that day and age, I cannot leave out Fire Rescue. I must say you could not ask for a better backup, or a more professionally trained department. These first-aid-trained firemen, in my estimation, like us, are the best in the United States. They performed lifesaving miracles on a daily basis and never failed to show up in a timely manner. We shared the utmost respect for each other. Therefore, when they needed a backup, we came at top speed. Together, we were an unbeatable team of lifesavers. Really something to see as we arrived ready to handle any emergency that could prove fatal. Time and skill were the essence for a lifesaving outcome, and together we got better with every life or death emergency, as previously mentioned. After we learned to call for Fire Rescue on our most serious runs, we did not feel alone. In the early 1970's, and years before EMS was conceived, we relied on their heavy units. These trucks were packed with medical supples and tactical emergency rescue gear. Even to this day, their crews are still expertly trained in any and all life-threatening occurrences. In my opinion, alongside with the D.P.D., the Detroit Fire Department is also Detroit's FINEST.

On rare occasions, when things were really busy, we would receive a call from a neighboring precinct. On one summer evening we got that run:

"17-3, make the 18th precinct, such and such location, a police officer has been shot, no other wagons available!"

"On the way, radio, 17-3!"

Now hop in and make this run with us. Lights and siren at top speed. We are pumped! Upon arriving at the scene of an apartment building, we found that someone had already transported the officer.

As we entered the lobby and the scene of the shooting, we learned that there had been an attempted hold up. Two males, high on heroin, decided to rob a man coming into the lobby with two arms of groceries. The one in front pulled a knife. The one in back of him held a gun. As the one in front went through the off-duty police officer's pockets, he exposed the officer's I.D. Knowing he had only one chance, the officer dropped the bags and pulled his 357 magnum. As he fired, the first round struck the holdup man in front under his chin exiting through the top of his head. He was deceased long before his body hit the floor.

The other assailant fired one round striking the officer who was already wheeling around to return several deadly rounds of hot lead. The wounded officer, with lethal precision, fired four rounds in self-defense, each round striking the armed felon. The high powered rounds went all the way through the perp, leaving four entry and four exit wounds.

The lobby was still filled with the smell of gun smoke when we made the scene. While the sergeant in the lobby explained to us how the scene played out, we heard a faint moan. To our amazement, the second gunman was still alive and trying to talk!

Just then, an 18th precinct wagon arrived and conveyed him to the hospital. We later learned that because he was so high, he never went into shock. Even more surprising is that he survived surgery!

Many conveyances later, we were assigned a brand new wagon. It was sky blue with gold colored lettering. Upon inspection, I learned it was no ordinary wagon. It was equipped with a heavy-duty suspension, a 440 magnum engine, and a top speed of 140 M.P.H.! I was in seventh heaven. My partner and I were the envy of the shift.

Chapter 11

SUNDAY MORNING HORROR

It was a quiet summer Sunday morning. Come along and take another ride with us…

We had just left the station ramp and decided to go for breakfast. As we sat down to order we heard these words, "13-4, we are getting a shooting, just happened, one shot at such and such address!"

We responded, "Okay, Dispatch 13-4 on the way!

Arriving at a wooden two-story structure, we were met by a citizen from the scene. Grabbing the stretcher, we ran up two flights of stairs!

Once there, we observed a grizzly scene of blood spattered almost everywhere in the room where the victim laid. He was moaning in pain, with a large hole in his chest and blood spurting. We knew we had to react fast. Putting him on the stretcher, we proceeded to carry him down the tricky two-flight stairway.

I was in front of the stretcher going down the stairs when warm blood began to run down and inside my uniform shirt. I ignored the horrible feeling, as I was bent on trying to save his life.

We finally got him secured in the wagon, put his wife in the back seat, while she tried to comfort him. I jumped behind the wheel, while my partner notified dispatch, "Radio 13-4 has the shooting victim. Notify DGH we are enroute, priority one!

Fortunately, the scene was not far from the freeway. When I entered the on ramp, I noticed the freeway was clear of traffic. As I made my way to the center lane, I checked the speedometer. It registered 90 MPH. At this point, I floored the new wagon: 100, 110, 120, I buried the speedometer at 140!

Our shooting victim was still conscious, as we backed up to the dock in under one and ½ minutes! The E.R. crew was already waiting, from our previous notification to dispatch.

Later, we felt elated, as again we had never lost a trauma patient. There were no arrests in this case as the shooting was totally accidental.

One day the inevitable happened. We were flagged down by several citizens who pointed out a woman down on the sidewalk. They said she was about seven months pregnant, had fallen, and had internal bleeding. Immediately, we put her on our stretcher and rushed her to the hospital, again in record time.

As we wheeled her into E.R., the doctor asked her what had happened. She said she had fallen and busted her lip! We were all speechless, because the citizens that flagged us down completely fooled us into thinking she had internal bleeding. With all of the priority one life and death runs, this one was not what it seemed. My partner and I realized that at least we still had a perfect record of a live patient conveyance!

12 Chapter
NEIGHBORHOOD BEAT

I was now reassigned back to a scout car and had learned enough to feel confident in teaching new recruits. I also had learned that if you were a law-abiding citizen, you loved us; if you were on the wrong side of the law, you loved to hate us! These strong emotions often implicated safety, or sometimes sparked deadly violence towards police officers. Unfortunately, more citizens observe us writing tickets or making arrests than those that saw us saving lives.

As previously mentioned, law enforcement had become known as a profession. To the majority of veteran police officers and their families, it is a way of life. When I swore allegiance to the Force, I took a $5,000 cut in pay, not including stock options. I knew that there would be no huge monetary gains. To some this would seem a financial disaster. However, in my bright and youthful mind, I felt whole heartedly that I could make a positive difference. This could be my way to serve my community and my country simultaneously. Besides, at this time in my life, money was of no consequence. I had no bills and my sport car and motorcycle were paid for.

I was in my early twenties and I had never felt so mentally alert. My visual acuity sharper and my body was physically strong. I knew that I could defend the defenseless, overpower those who loved to prey on the weak; and even protect other police officers from unfair supervision and dangerous criminals. Yes, I even dared to protect police officers of the DPD! To be truthful, there were some officers that I could not stand the sight of. However, you can be sure that if we were working together, when we left that ramp we watched each other's back until the end of the shift. We knew that the criminals never make a distinction when they mean you harm. All they see is blue!

It is very hard to explain to the laymen the feeling of wearing a target for a uniform; or sitting in a possible death trap, your scout car, or the feeling of drawing fire from an ambush at anytime, anywhere. You can only rely on your training and discipline, or being able to read your partner's mind knowing every move he or she will make.

My partner and I decided to make our scout car area safe. Even in those days we knew this to be more than a notion. We made our minds up to be determined and immune to the additional danger that no one asked of us. We put together a plan to hunt the local career criminals who preyed on their neighbors and the defenseless citizens of the neighborhood.

Our tactic was to create an environment where the worst of the thugs and felons became the prey. To be hunted and pounced upon in your own neighborhood at any given time was not only unnerving but proved that the bullies could not take what they dished out. They did not want to receive one scratch, or have one hair on their heads harmed.

Remember, our street training proved that in order to be effective, let alone survive the criminal world, you must be stronger, smarter, extremely tougher, and learn the way they think. Don't get it wrong; some felons are extremely cunning. Some will probably end up reading this book. Therefore, I have left out what might be detrimental to us or you my public. The covert and deadly street tactics that I and my senior partners have learned must be taught to officers only.

I must tell you that I have been threatened by some of the worst that the streets have to offer. To those that expressed a need and want to kill my partner and me, we put them on notice that if and when we ever saw them again, we would react as though they were attempting to carry out that threat and would respond accordingly. This is no game and we had learned to be deadly serious. What was more chilling is that they knew we meant every word.

Meanwhile, a change started to take place in the neighborhood. The children started playing outside again, after school, and on the weekends. The elderly began to come out, sitting on porches and taking walks. They invited us on their porches and in their homes. That winter we were the first crew ever to receive Christmas cards sent to the precinct station. I wish I had kept them. We knew the criminals hated us for doing our job. But they respected the fact that this was now our turf, and we protected it like it was a child. It got to the point that we would park our cruiser and walk the neighborhood like beat officers. We almost had celebrity status, almost!

Chapter 13

A BIZARRE SCENE

Meanwhile, back on the beat…

One summer day right after roll call and off the ramp, we received a police run to H.P.P.D. (Highland Park Police Department). A city surrounded by Detroit.

When we arrived at the station, an officer pointed out a woman and a teenage male. As we sat down, the teen began to tell a story too chilling to believe, but the details were too accurate to disbelieve!

This bizarre scene started with several 15-year-olds who decided to skip school. They went to one teen's home were the parents were not present.

As they sat around in the living room trying to think of something to do, the teen's older, uninvited brother walked in. He was 18 and had just been released from jail. He suggested that they play a game. Disappearing for a moment, he returned with a handgun and said, "We are going to play a game called Russian roulette!"

The girls and boys just sat there puzzled about what he meant. Just then, he pulled back the hammer and pointed the gun at one of the teens. When he pulled the trigger the gun fired, striking one of the young boys in the chest. The teen fell forward onto the floor.

Everyone was frozen in horror, except the 18-year-old that left briefly and came back with a rug. He never attempted first aid, or called 911.

He simply said, "Help me roll him up in this rug."

My partner and I were stunned. We questioned the youth about the location of this possible shooting scene. He could not remember the address, but gave us the street name and cross streets.

We notified dispatch that we were going to another precinct for further investigation.

While enroute to the neighboring precinct, we switched radio frequencies and requested to have a scout car meet us at the location. We put the woman and her son in the scout car and headed for the location. We told them to remain in the car.

When the crew arrived, we stood in front of the suspect's house and informed the backup of the situation. I suggested that we first check the garage, since this is where our witness said the perp had put the body in a garbage can.

I had one of the officers come with me to check the garage, before we called for homicide squad and obtained a search warrant. We did not need a search warrant to check the garage, as the door was already ajar.

As I opened the garage door, the first thing I noticed was a small trail of blood. Opening the door wider, we saw a garbage can! We were shocked. There was a rug rolled up in the can. Protruding from the rug were the blue jean covered legs wearing tennis shoes. The child's body was upside down in the can!

Meanwhile, the 15-year-old brother of the killer had opened the front door. He told my partner and the other officer that his brother was half a block away playing cards! While my partner and I made notifications and held the scene, the other crew went down the block to make the arrest. As supervision and other police officers arrived, we turned the homicide scene and the witness over to them and left for our precinct to complete our report. It was one of our more depressing homicide scenes. The whole episode was surreal. We were in another zone.

Chapter 14

INNOCENT CHILDREN IN DANGER

It was another warm summer day in Detroit. Even with 6000 plus police officers, there was still an abundance of police work to perform

One of our crews radioed, "Dispatch. This is 17-6. We have a man shooting at children. He is now barricaded in his apartment. We need back up and a supervisor!"

Radio responded, "I can send you back up, but no supervisor available!"

17-6 responded, "Well, can you send 13-4?"

I responded, "We are okay on that and on the way, radio!"

Some of the other scout car crews in our precinct had come to rely our knowledge in tough street situations. I felt this was a part of my responsibility to help other officers as well as citizens.

We responded with priority one speed and were met by one of my frantic precinct officers who gave us a quick rundown.

My partner and I were determined not to let this turn into a spectacle. We grabbed our heavy gear, including a long gun, and prepared to resolve the situation quickly. Clearing the area of citizens, we prepared for a possible gun battle.

Shouting into the hall were the gunman was held up, "Detroit Police. Throw your weapon into the hall. You have 30 seconds, or we will come in shooting!"

Just then, one of the gunman's neighbors walked up to us. He begged us to let him talk to the man, because he knew him quite well.

I told him, "Okay, you tell him I want him to back out of the apartment hands up, no weapon!"

The neighbor went in. Within seconds, he and the perp backed out with their hands up. We made the arrest. I instructed the original crew to confiscate his weapon, a shotgun. Just then, a sergeant arrived on scene. He asked, "Who is in charge here?"

I shouted, "I am, Sarge!"

"Who gave you permission to handle this scene?"

I told him that I was requested, as there were no supervisors available; and that this was a potentially explosive scene, with shots fired at children. Because of hostile parents, I decided to act quickly.

He shook his head and said, "I'm glad it worked out." As he walked away he replied, "Good police work, officers!"

We were pleased that we took the gunman alive. However, because of the seriousness of the crime, we were quite prepared to use extreme deadly force. We felt that if he would shoot at children he would shoot anyone.

Chapter 15

WHICH WAY DID HE GO? WHICH WAY DID HE GO?

One particular day all seemed quiet, as we slowly patrolled the streets on the north end. We decided to stop for lunch, as we were invited into a citizen's home.

Almost as soon as we sat down a chase came over the air. It was a motorcycle. Thinking it would be over shortly, we decided to continue our lunch. However, halfway through our lunch not only were they still chasing the bike, but it was getting close to our location. Now, we began to pay more attention. I said, "Let's go and get this guy!" We called back in.

As we listened over the mobile, we made a right turn heading south since we heard he was northbound on the same street.

Suddenly, the rider approached. We veered to avoid him. But he kept coming. To our surprise, he came straight for us! We collided and the bike was impaled on the push bumper. Push bumpers are steel rods about 1-1/2" in diameter. There are two of them that are bolted to the frame. They were made to push or ram vehicles. Their round structure made them very durable. They were painted a shiny black.

The rider had disappeared. We didn't know what had happened to him. I looked in my rear view mirror and there he was, standing behind the scout car facing north - the same way he was riding!

We exited the vehicle and the driver seemed puzzled as to how he had ended up there. Numerous scout cars that were chasing him began pulling up amazed at what they were seeing.

I walked up to the fugitive and asked if he was okay? Still seeming stunned he said, "Yes."

We figured out that when we hit he did a complete somersault over the entire scout car and landed on his feet! The bike was stuck on the push bumper with a hole through the crankcase. We asked him why he was fleeing and he said, "My driver's license was suspended."

We placed him under arrest, while we waited for a tow truck for his bike. Our precinct had a good reputation for catching almost everyone that we chased in a vehicle.

16 Chapter
SMART-MOUTH DRIVER

I know that one of the public's dislike for police officers derives from traffic tickets. This is one undisputable problem drivers have with the police. You may not agree with me, however, it is a necessary and much needed law. I had worked out a formula that seemed to work rather well. I'll let you be the judge.

As a professional officer, we were instructed to always approach a driver with a, "Hello sir, or mam. Can I see your driver's license and registration, Please?"

At this juncture, I would let the driver's response to my request make my decision as to whether I would issue an ordinance or not. For instance, if I were met with a "What the "F#@@, did you stop me for?" Or, "Haven't you got anything better to do?" Automatic ticket. Or, if I was greeted cordially, I would return with their paperwork, a slight warning, and a have a nice day! Surprisingly, I would get so many negative or threatening responses that I could literally run out of tickets! Here again, just making a simple traffic stop was not routine. It could be deadly, with several occupants or just one.

On a lighter note: every now and then, with all of the excuses you will hear, there are rare times that will astound you.

I was working with a rookie one fall afternoon. We were driving in traffic when I noticed the vehicle in front of us. Every time he stopped in this older vehicle his brake lights did not function. After a short distance, I signaled for him to pull over and told my partner to handle the traffic stop. I was watching his back when I noticed him conversing back and forth with the driver. He came back to the car shaking his head and told me I should talk to the citizen. I approached the driver. "Good afternoon, sir! Did you know your brake lights are not working?"

"Yes," he responded, "I know. I loaned them to my neighbor!"

"What do you mean, you loaned them to your neighbor," I asked?

With a serious face, he explained that his neighbor had the same make and model car as his, and his brake lights went out so he loaned him his brake light switch!

Knowing this had to be the truth and trying not to laugh, I told him, "Okay, sir. You may go!"

As I entered the scout car, my partner and I had quite a laugh. It made our day!

By the same token, on another day I was working a one-man car 13-41, which could only be done on days, because of the danger. I happened to pull over a vehicle for speeding and a varying course of travel without a signal.

As I approached the vehicle, I noticed there were six occupants. When I requested a driver's license and registration from the driver, someone in the rear seat shouted, "Why did you stop us?"

I told him I was talking to the driver. There was another negative comment shouted.

At this point, I ordered everyone out of the car. I told all of them to put their hands on the trunk of the vehicle they were riding in. One smart mouth shouted, "There's six of us and only one of you!"

I told him, "I see you did not do well in school with math!" There's actually seven of us: six 44 magnum slugs and me!"

He said, "Oh S@#T, don't shoot!"

I responded, "Like I said, I've been trying to tell you to shut up. I'm talking to the driver!" Then I added, "Driver, step back here with me and give me your driver's license and registration; and one more word from the math major and it's an automatic ticket!" His crew suddenly understood that the threat was real and everything went well.

17 Chapter

NO BACKING DOWN

I have learned that backing down from a creditable threat can be dangerous, especially when there is a crowd involved.

On a late summer evening, on the afternoon shift, we received a run on the north end of the precinct. "17-3, a disturbance at such and such address, unknown on the weapons!"

"On the way, Radio 17-3!" (From-time-to-time, our regular scout car would not be available due to repairs, oil changes, or tire changes, so we drove what was available.)

When we arrived, we saw a large crowd in the middle of the street. We did not know what the disturbance was about, but there was one man agitating the crowd.

Pulling up across from the crowd, we asked them to disperse.

The one man instigating the crowd said, "Don't listen to them. Let's get them!"

Recognizing the fact that we would have to weed out the trouble maker, with my hand on my gun, I said, "You, with the big mouth, you are under arrest. Step forward."

He replied, "What are you going to do; shoot me?"

Realizing he was trying to provoke me in front of numerous witnesses and to back down would cause further aggression from the crowd, I remembered I had a large knife taken in a previous run. Pulling out the large knife, I said, "No, but I will cut you!"

The perp instantly froze.

I waved the knife for him to come forward, as he pleaded, "Please don't cut me. I give up!"

A hush came over the crowd. They watched intently, while I held the large knife on him and my partner cuffed the man. I told the crowd to go home. We waited for them to disperse and left with our arrest.

18 Chapter
DON'T MESS WITH THESE SENIORS

This next incident is rather complicated, so I will set it up for you.

One summer evening, around the first of the month, a group of senior citizens gathered to play cards as they did every month.

Unknown to the harmless seniors, three punks from the hood became aware of this social get together and decided to descend upon the unsuspecting old timers. Their plan was simple, although not very bright, but to them it was ingenious.

There were three of them. They would use as their only weapon: one 22 caliber six-shot revolver. The plan was to rob the seniors of the money on the card table then torture them to get any additional money that might be hidden.

They went up to the third floor, knocked on the door pretending to be an old timer, and were let in. Right away the one with the only weapon pulled the gun, while the other two collected the money.

Now here is where the greed came in. They wanted any other money that was not in sight.

To make the seniors talk, the one with the gun would strike each one in the head with the butt of the gun discharging a non-penetrating shot, which terriorized the seniors even more. However, the seniors were no chumps like their adversaries and still would not talk.

The perps seemed to be having a good time, but failed to realize the mathematical equation that suggests that after six shots the gun was empty. Therefore, on the seventh pull of the trigger, the weapon went CLICK! It was the loudest sound in the apartment for the thugs.

As I previously mentioned, the old timers were no one's chumps. The second they heard the gun's hammer fall on an empty chamber two of them moved to block the door.

In the apartment, was an old-style triangular steel jack tower used to jack up old five to six thousand pound full-size cars!

The gunman panicked first. He ran to the kitchen and jumped out of the window. The second broke for the only door and was met with a blow to the head with the three-foot jack tower. The third decided to fight. He was struck several times so hard that the tip of the jack penetrated his chest.

I would imagine that a matter of minutes later is where we came in!

"13-4, we are getting an attempted armed robbery in progress; perpetrators still at the scene!"

"Radio 13-4 is on the way!"

When we arrived at the scene, it was relatively quiet outside. We went up to the third floor where an elderly gentleman let us in. His head was bleeding and he was holding a towel to his wound.

As we entered the apartment, we saw about six other men and women with head wounds. We also noticed a man on the floor and one on the couch bleeding from the chest.

The older man began to tell us what you have just read. As I took notes, my partner called dispatch and requested several E.M.S. units.

Still taking notes, something struck me as very odd. Then it came to me. Where was the third man?

I went into the kitchen, looked out of the window, and there he was lying in a stairwell. To his misfortune, in addition to falling three stories, there was a metal guard rail next to the basement steps. He had hit them all!

About this time, the first aid crews had arrived and were treating the old timers. We had to call for two additional units for the mathematical wizards who also forgot to count the fact that they were on the third floor before one of them jumped!

As we exited the apartment building, we were surprised to find a large hostile crowd had gathered. We quickly learned that the crowd knew the punks but not the victims.

Now to show how suddenly a situation can occur, the crowd had decided that the police had beaten the punks. Now they were the victims and we were the bad guys. There were five E.M.S. units at this scene trying to administer first aid to nine injured people.

My partner and I were trying to contain the most aggressive participants of the crowd. One heckler disobeyed and came into the street yelling orders for us to attend to his friend, one of the holdup men.

I warned him to return to the sidewalk. When I walked toward the first aid units, he followed closely behind me. I felt his finger poke me in the back. Instinctively, I turned and struck the heckler. As he fell, I noticed I had his shirt in my fist.

My sergeant said I should leave the scene, because of the crowd; but I noticed they had calmed down.

To secure our prisoners, my partner and I followed E.M.S. to the hospital. This time it was a good day for the innocent.

Chapter 19
SEEING IN THE DARK

It was a nippy fall evening. We were assigned to the northwest section of our precinct. Now ride with us if you dare, as we patrolled this potentially dangerous sector…

We received a police run: "13-3; make such and such a location. We are getting this run as a B&E in progress!"

Allow me to set this situation up for you, just to show how lethal the police occupation was and still remains to be.

As I have mentioned in the past, police partners learn to think like twins and have a M.O. for just about any situation worked out.

Instead of a B&E, what was actually taking place was a hold up in progress in the downstairs section of a two-family flat. The downstairs occupant had received his income tax check. Somehow, a couple of local hold up men had learned about it. They had forced entry. One was armed with a handgun and the other with a sawed off rifle.

"On the way, Radio 13-3 responding from two blocks away!"

Now, there is one other unknown danger to this life-threatening event, when we get a run that is in progress and we are only seconds away. Just imagine the collision between good and evil in such close proximity.

As we pulled up to the scene, my partner went down one side of the building and I the other side. Both reaching the rear at the same time and finding nothing we returned to the front, not knowing that the two hold up men were watching us through a slit in the curtain. The occupant suddenly opened the front door and said, "They just robbed me and ran out the back door!"

My partner broke for the backyard instantly and had a slight lead on me. The R.A. man with the handgun had already disappeared. The second perp had just jumped the back fence leading to the alley.

As I pulled my weapon, the perp turned to take a shot at my partner. Because I was taller, I was able to fire my 44 magnum over my partner before the felon could get off a shot. A flame emerged six feet from my barrel and lit the area like daylight. The subject went down. Relieved that I had protected my partner, we were about to jump the fence when the felon jumped up and ran. As he made the corner of a garage, I got off two more shots. Wood flew off of the garage just behind him. I jumped the fence and my partner called in for back up, giving a description and a direction of escape. As I emerged, moving in the footsteps of the escapee, for the first time overhead was a Detroit police chopper. Its first radio designation was AIR ONE!

It was gratifying to know that I had eyes in the night sky. I gave out further information and watched as the air unit responded to my prep radio. All of a sudden it came over the radio, "We've got him." It was a block away from my location!

As I approached the scene, I could hear a man screaming, "Don't let that officer shoot at me again. I give up!" The officer that found the felon told me that when he was searching the area, he heard the sound of rattling coming from under a parked car and the perp still ranting the same plea!

After we read him his rights, he confessed and even gave up his partner. It just wasn't his time to die, or my partner's. It also proved that a deadly 44 magnum could save lives as well.

Chapter 20

COMMUNITY AND NEIGHBORS WORKING TOGETHER

At roll call one afternoon, the sergeant read off a teletype involving two prostitutes that went rogue and started robbing their customers. One was armed with a blue steel semi-automatic; the other a knife. This was a priority B.O.L. The sergeant feared sooner or later, they would kill one of the Johns.

The descriptions of the prosttutes were somewhat vague. They fit most of the street walkers.

My partner and I went on the prowl, as these incidents were occurring in our scout car area.

Day after day, no trace. We felt this was unusual. They seemed to have vanished. Perhaps they knew the heat was on.

Much later, while on patrol, we were hailed by one of the ladies of the evening. She seemed frantic, asked us to pull around the corner out of sight, and explained to us that these two hold up women were bad for business because there were too many police around. Then she told us she knew where we could find one of them right now; giving a description and a location.

We took off right away to the spot she indicated. Sure enough, the info was accurate. There she was standing midblock in broad daylight, hands on her hips, a large purse swinging from one arm. Her body language told us she was not to be taken lightly.

We made a plan to use a surprise attack from behind. We approached her blind side and grabbed both arms, "You are under arrest for armed robbery and felonious assault."

She went wild, as my partner put one cuff on her wrist. She kicked him between the legs. He was down. She then attempted to strike me with the flailing cuff dangling from her other wrist. When she swung, I avoided the attack and struck her with one left hook. She dropped like a wet rag, unconscious. I cuffed her and called for first aid for my partner. This particular felon was the one with the knife. After interrogation by the precinct detectives, she gave up her partner in crime.

Everyone would like to enjoy safe streets and a safe community. However, that reality is going to take just that: a community working together - neighbors actively looking out for each other and knowing your neighbors' schedules and habits.

I'm not leaving the police out, because this kind of neighborly organization promotes police effectiveness in taking down would be criminals in our neighborhood.

As we all know, freedom is not free! The need for a police officer in today's society is greater than ever before. Therefore, the public needs to know that we will stop at nothing to protect them from the worst criminal element; and putting your lives before our own in the process.

You must understand that we know that adults need a hero just as well as our children; and have a right not to have to live in fear.

Chapter 21

TEAMWORK: POLICE AND FIRE DEPARTMENTS WORKING TOGETHER

There is a history between the Detroit Police and the Detroit Fire Department. For years, since the early 70's, we both began to work without the needed equipment to fight crime and fires, knowing that both departments were in the life-saving business.

In the early 2000's, on a visit from New York, the N.Y.F.D. had occasion to watch the D.F.D. in action; doing what they do best – efficiently battling some of the worst fires with little equipment. They remarked that they had never seen anything like it, and that it was a learning experience that they could take home.

In 1977, when the first Detroit police layoffs occurred, because of a labor contract dispute between the mayor and the police union, big city recruiters came from all over the U.S. to grab our laid off officers, like a number one draft pick! They were told that their street experience was of combat quality and they would not be required to go through their academy. Even the F.B.I. waived their two-year college qualification for Detroit police officers for the same reason, that deadly street expertise!

Let's not forget, however, that experience has come at a costly price over numerous years. My cause was to remember to defend the rights of all citizens and lawful police officers, even until retirement, which means there is no such thing as an ex-policeman.

Also keep in mind our loved ones often find it hard to understand what is heroic about our dying.

Early in the beginning of my career, my father made me promise that he would not have to identify me in the morgue. That is the main purpose of this written work: to continue to save lives and to survive to do so.

There is no logical reason why we should die trying to uphold the law; but there are those who hate the very ground we walk upon.

Chapter 22

A FEW SURVIVAL SKILLS

Several years ago there was a house full of unsupervised teens and several little ones under the influence of the older teens. This was in my neighborhood and, as usual, I have experienced this over the years. They were told that I was an officer. They had not lived there a week before they started disrupting the entire block: standing in the street, blocking traffic, smoking weed out in the open in front of the toddlers in broad daylight, boxing and wrestling mid street, cussing, intimidating mothers and children walking by. After a while, since they didn't even go to school, they started breaking into the homes right on the block where they lived. They threatened a woman visiting a neighbor so aggressively that the man in the house came out with a gun to kill them. I regret that I stopped him.

It was just a matter of time before they started in on me. I warned them, that as much as they thought they hated me, one day they would need my help. They walked away puzzled. I never said they were "A" students.

Sure enough, one day they angered the wrong people who came in the night with guns. The tougher gang fired several shots up their driveway and the young punks screamed bloody murder for the police. They even had the nerve to run onto my porch for safety; proving again that bullies are just scared punks and thugs who do not want to get hurt.

It is a fact that without police officers even these hoodlums would not stand a chance in the streets. They would never survive. So why do they want to kill the police? Simply put, they have no respect for life, limb, or property, no breeding, or home training. They also know that we stand for the wellbeing of the people and when it gets too hot for them, the same ones who would kill us call for our protection! Ironically pitiful isn't it? And, since they need us so badly, it is imperative that we survive, because we are the invisible thin line between law and order and total anarchy.

This survival begins with police officers practicing situation awareness. Learn your neighborhoods and your precinct's surroundings, and never search a person while sitting in your cruiser. It is dangerous to allow a potential suspect to step up to your scout car where you can reach his or her pockets checking for a weapon. As a result of this, one of our officers was shot in the face by a suspect in my scout car area. Be capable of pulling your weapon while in your car. Know what you and your partner will do in a life and death situation. Know (what we called in Detroit) your "Delta areas," (high crime area or a danger to a police). These locations should and must be of great concern to you and your citizenry. Know your scout car, inside and out. Be capable of operating your cruiser's offensive and defensive characteristics, including high speed and cruising speed maneuvers and when and where not to use overheads and sirens. These are just a very few of what I call "street survival skills;" and be ready for an ambush type of attack at all times. These ambush attacks are what your nemesis practice, as they use them on defenseless citizens every day.

Let's start now to turn our fatality statistics around in favor of the peace officer.

Chapter 23

A FRIGHTENING BUT TRUE STATISTIC

Just as in life, it seems to be the best of us that are slaughtered. One would ask, "Where do these violent criminals come from?

In my experience, a whole host of negative environments have a profound effect on a young child. Dysfunctional families are abundant in today's society. In order to bring a child up straight, you must start at the beginning with the very young. Past a certain age of abuse or neglect, that child becomes a product of its surroundings, usually with a negative outlook on life, the future, and you.

This is only a part of the grim picture. Couple that background with a gang of negative peers. Just use your imagination. Picture this fact for example: take a child that has never learned to read. I know that seems mind boggling in today's society, however, it is very real and happening every day. The extraordinary result is a child, a teen or young adult that lives in a separate world from you and me, a lonely, chilling and subdued place where they are completely alienated by the thought of education. Reading, out of the question, math the same, writing no clue, socializing with their learned peers, not likely. Every day their world grows smaller. As technical advances accelerate, they are left in a void that grows larger just as rapidly. What is the eventuality?

Over 90 % of them will end up in prison. Frightening, but true. Now they have become students of the prison system. When and if they are released back into society, what are they faced with? Can our learning technology help in any way, or has our advanced civilization failed them? Is there a solution in quantum physics that can be fed into a super computer for the institutionalized masses? Or, finally, should we start building private prisons to house what may become over half of our country's population?

24 Chapter

PAVING THE WAY

Long before the State Police graced Detroit freeways, there was an elite section called Motor Traffic. This motorized unit consisted of high performance scout cars, white in color with black lettering. For the surface streets, the department used Harley Davidson motorcycles. These officers specialized in high speed, high performance driving in all traffic conditions. Some of their other specialties were accidents, ticket writing, motorcade escorts, funeral traffic (often hazardous), and police chases.

These one-man cars each patrolled one of the cities freeways and handled anything freeway related. I was completely mesmerized by their almost stunt car abilities with these two types of motor vehicles. I witnessed a motor man on the freeway ram a totaled out vehicle that was in an accident with his push bumpers and shove it onto the shoulder to clear traffic.

These officers were one with both types of vehicles, totally impressive. The scout cars were capable of 140 M.P.H. plus. They were also very adept at pouncing on reckless drivers on the ditch, (a police term for the freeway) closing on them very rapidly, most times from a parked position. This was made possible by big block powertrains from Detroit auto makers know how. This is the same auto industry that became known as the legendary Arsenal of Democracy during WWII and put the world on wheels.

The Detroit Police Department also has a rich history, becoming the first police department in the State of Michigan back in the year 1865. The D.P.D spawned many firsts in its infancy and beyond. They were the first to use bicycles and motorcycles. They were the first to put mobile radios in scout cars, carry prep radio outfits, to incorporate the four-man heavy cruiser, (known as The Big Four) to arrest the toughest of criminals, to invent Community Oriented Patrol, (C.O.P.) small motorcycles to respond to minor police runs, and give transparency in the neighborhoods. There are more firsts to be mentioned later. D.P.D. has been and remains a very innovative entity in this city and the nation and has a genuine interest in shoring up its sometimes negative image. And, yes, we officer do care!

Back in the day, every year in the month of May, all Detroit police precincts participated in Police Week. We would put out a display in the precinct lobby of various police-related objects and paraphernalia, pull several scout cars into the garage where a police officer would pack the car with children. Naturally, their favorite attraction was Lights and Sirens. We would take them on tours into the cell block area, empty of prisoners of course. There were hotdogs, pop, popcorn, and other treats for the citizens.

Once a year, there was the Police Field Day celebration, or should I call it a demonstration? This was a show unlike any other. The tickets were very cheap, but the entertainment was rich with skilled police stunts, maneuvers, and mounted division's highly-trained horse shows. And, let's not forget, the D.P.D. canine units trained German Shepherds. All of these thrills and spectacles for a few dollars per ticket. It was a milestone in my early days on the force. I wish those community-friendly attractions could be restored. It was like Christmas in the summer for the children. To see the excitement on their faces made our efforts more than worthwhile. We definitely had a more cohesive bond with the community, and it showed when we cruised the neighborhoods. We were super heroes to the children and guardians of their parents and neighbors.

There are no monetary riches in police work and, for the first time, the politicians have bypassed the Michigan Constitution and taken part of our Pensions that we shed our blood, sweat, and money to build up. I won't go any further with this for it is too emotional; especially for those of us that are disabled in the line of duty. However, some of us do find riches from the love of the job and the love of the community and city that we protect.

Being a native son of Detroit, I find it to be many things: industrial, multi-lingual, ethnic and exploding with history. Also a center for many interests: nature, cultural, sports, entertainment, educational, technology, innovative inventor's center, a humane society center for animals, and a charitable humanitarian center. For those people, as well as our furry friends, Detroit is full of angels of mercy, many of them anonymous. In my opinion, they stand out more than most other cities; and for the frail and helpless, a true blessing!

Chapter 25

COMMUNICATIONS DEPARTMENT

Before there was a 911 Emergency Medical System (EMS), Detroit police officers took emergency calls in a specialized section called Communications sanctioned by the Federal Communications Commission (F.C.C.) Our air waves were constantly monitored for the continuous high standards of the rules set forth by the commission. The rules were so strict that dispatchers must announce the time in military terms every fifteen minutes, starting on the hour with letter and number codes. These codes identify the D.P.D. radio station to the F.C.C. for further monitoring of our license.

As a matter of fact, we had two such radio stations. Late in the 1960's, this operation was revamped, and in the early 1970's the 911 system was born in Detroit. The sixth floor of Police Headquarters, known as 1300 Beaubien, was infused with numerous personnel: civilians for 911 and newly transferred police officers for dispatch.

There were several large metal consoles: four of them for the four zones, containing several precincts for each zone; one large console for L.I.E.N and N.C.I.C. checks, manned by four officers, and one huge console mid floor called the Communications Chief Operators Console (CHO). This position was a high priority at the time and was only assigned to top seniority officers. The other one-third of the room was sectioned off by a glass wall and was occupied by the 911 Operators. This now meant that the new Communications Chief Operators ConsoleSection (C.O.S.) was now the largest of its kind in the world. Another DPD first!

There were several additional consoles that could be made operational quickly in case of a shut down. These C.O.S. technical leaps were overseen by Belle Isle radio experts; some were WWII vets, also known as the Greatest Generation. Their electronic, telecommunications, and radio skills put this new operation ahead by leaps and bounds. In the event of any technical difficulty, or system shut down, they were readily available 24/7. Their contributions were invaluable!

As the years went, by this section was visited frequently by police departments from all over the world. It was a prestigious time in Communications history. Every year, as small kinks were worked out, this section became more efficient by rapidly passing info from a 911 phone call to the officers on the street walking up to the scene of the call. Technology continued to advance rapidly. Electronics inside of these metal consoles produced heat, which is an enemy to electronic circuits. To combat this condition, central air was pumped into the consoles from under the floor - problem eradicated.

Security on this floor was top notch; no one could gain entry without being monitored on closed circuit camera, conversing by speaker, and finally being cleared by the officer on the super console, the C.H.O.

We did not know it at the time, but the DPD dispatchers were the absolute power behind city-wide communications and directors of all scout car activities, bringing Fire and EMS under our umbrella of protection. It is unfortunate that these two life-saving entities would often times need police protection in order to do their jobs, saving lives. One year, firemen were being shot at while trying to put out fires. The dispatchers quickly stomped out this practice by sending one scout car crew with each fire company.

By early 2000, it was discovered that our 911 system was taking more calls than the city of New York, which has over nine times our population. I have been told that statistic still exists.

Our second radio station was strictly reserved for the suburban police departments that surrounded our borders and beyond. This radio was exclusively operated by the CHO operator. This was just one of the many responsibilities of the senior officer. He could notify any of the local police departments of any bank robbers, hold up suspects, rapists, arsonists, B&E suspects, high speed chases, or any other serious criminals crossing into their borders. Likewise, they could notify this officer of any felony or misdemeanor suspects headed our way. This was a grand marriage. The cooperation between our cities was stupendous and the coordination produced an invisible dragnet that almost no crook could escape. Because of the advance radio communication between us, when they crossed the city limits, going from or coming to Detroit, we set up a predatory trap and sprang it.

These were the old days, over four decades ago, just to give you an idea of what our WWII coworkers devised. By the late 1970's, most of them had retired and we baby boomers picked up the pace as we stood on the shoulders of those giants!

Upon further examination, this practice made perfect logic; who else could understand the workings of life in the streets and melt minds with the officers; knowing how they thought and what they felt. In addition, a Communications officer had to know the city, its streets, its addresses, precinct boundaries, and city limits.

Another practice that was strictly Communications protocol was in the event a C.O.S. officer was promoted; he or she remained in their respective command. This was an ingenious practice, as it took years of training to make a seasoned dispatcher who could work at any position and dispatch cars anywhere in the city. Therefore, in order to supervise these highly skilled officers, it took one to supervise one and so on up the supervisory ladder. This was also necessary, because dispatchers had to give orders and police runs to any and all supervisors on the street at any given time. Sometimes those orders came right down the chain of command from our top supervision on the floor. A good dispatcher also knows that he or she might be sending a scout car crew to a possible fatal run. Therefore, the dispatcher also knows they must send them with all pertinent info, equipment, and back up so that they do survive!

26 Chapter
DISPATCH

The department led the way in police radio communications as well. In 1921, Commissioner William P. Rutledge became one of the first Police Executives in the country to foresee the use of the radio as a crime fighting tool, and Detroit became the first police department in the country to successfully put a radio-equipped police car into service. The system was created by Officers Bernard Fitzgerald, Walter Vogler, and Robert Batts....... all radio Hobbyists. By 1928, the Radio Broadcasting System was in full operation. (Detroit Free Press, May 7, 1987)

In the 1970's, Detroit issued battery powered radios known as P.R.E.P.S. These portable radios have saved many lives over the years. The Metropolitan Police Commission of Detroit was established in 1865 by an act of State Legislature and the Detective Bureau in 1866.

In the early 1970's, and years before, a Detroit Police Officer needed more than five year's street experience to transfer to communications. After the transfer, it could take six months to a year to turn a new officer into a rookie dispatcher.

There is considerable logic behind the necessary street experience it takes to make a qualified dispatcher. First, it helps to know the city, it's boundaries, streets and freeways, names and locations, to know how a police radio works and how to use it, radio codes, police codes, precinct locations and phone numbers, emergency contacts, how to effectively use your scout cars and police manpower, to give orders to even your superiors officers, handle life and death emergencies, and keep your officers safe until their watch is over.

Sounds intimidating and overwhelming? Well, it can be and it is. Not every officer makes the grade. My first experience on the other side of the radio was a horror story, until my street knowledge took over. Once I became comfortable on the air, I decided to make changes.

For a moment, let me take you out of the scout car and give you a mental action tour of DPD's brain child, the C.O.S. (Communications Operation Section) sitting at the controls of a console that is wired to dispatch several precincts at one time. I lovingly called it sitting in the electric chair, especially in the summer when radio air traffic was non-stop. My bright ideas started when I visualized my years of making the most dangerous police runs in the country.

In those days, roll call could fill our gym with police officers, (Roll call- where officers stood in formation for attendance and assignments). There were so many scout cars in each precinct that 3 or 4 or more police cars made the scene of all mild to serious police runs. This had an unnerving effect on the trouble makers and criminals of that era. Understanding that instead of patrolling one square scout car area, I was now protecting the lives of all of the citizens and police officers in three precincts, with some new and younger officers on the streets.

I decided to customize my scout car crews to the severity of the police runs. When a police run with guns was involved and depending on if it was a Delta Area, I would dispatch 3 to 4 scout cars. On a good day, a dispatcher will have a large fleet of scout cars crews under his or her command.

Next, I endeavored to know where my crews were whenever possible. At first the feeling was, if I knew where and what they were doing, that I would give them extra work. Over time, talking to all of the officers, I explained what I was trying to accomplish was for their own safety. Example: One of my 30 series UC cars (UC for undercover plain car, officers in plain clothes or plain and plain), called me over a secure phone and informed me that an informant relayed info of a big drug buy that was going to take place in a motel room. Ordinarily, before I introduced my plans, this two-man crew would have secretly tried to do this drug bust alone.

Because this crew now understood that my insisting on knowing about their freelance activities was not to impede them, but to enhance their good police work and safety, they were on board with me. I told them: "Here is what is going to happen. I am going to have three uniformed marked scout cars meet with you for a briefing at a staging area of your choosing. When you make your assault, I want you surrounded by uniformed officers." Later, I received a phone call from my 30 series that told me that the drug buyers and dealers gang were both heavily armed with guns. Because they had the overwhelming element of surprise, the perpetrators were outgunned and taken into custody without a shot being fired. Drugs and money confiscated, every officer went home safe. This made my day in the electric chair (smile).

As time went on, using these innovative ideas, my police crews got better and better. And to this very day, as I encounter some retired and some still active police officers, they tell me when they went on duty and heard my voice, they knew they were safe.

Another innovation was fitting certain crews to the specific tasks where they excelled: ie, some were good at spotting occupied stolen cars, some at high speed chases, some at patrolling Delta Areas, some at hunting wanted criminals, and some of my more seasoned crews just struck fear in the hearts and activities of career criminals, (those who commit crime after crime). For the ultimate danger, shots fired or an officer in trouble, I would send my personal hand-picked gun crews. These officers were fire teams experienced in gun fights. They were my first line of defense in all out street warfare in life and death police runs. The faster they arrived at an active scene, the better the chances of survival for police officers and citizens.

Every officer realizes that they are encompassed in a world of danger. It is both humbling and overwhelming to know that the sound of a dispatcher's voice in the night or day could bring such a feeling of safety and comfort to these men and women in blue. Once they leave that police station, the dispatcher is their only life line.

Now, I had three precincts, all of the citizens, all of the police officers, firemen and EMS to keep safe. On the force, just about everything worked by seniority. When I finally advanced to the CHO position, I had 25 years on the job. Talk about police experience, imagine that I had enough time for full retirement when I moved up to this top position. This is why police officers, including some from Scotland

Yard, came from all over the world to tour our operation in America. My main goal was not to impede my cars from effective police work but to enhance their ability to fight crime.

27 Chapter

MY DOORMAN EXPERIENCE

My first encounter with the Doorman occurred when I was still a rookie. I trained with a senior officer for several days before I took over. It was a demanding and dangerous job. As I found out later, you were on your feet for the whole shift except for a 30-minute lunch. There was a small table used for processing and finger printing, and a narrow hallway leading from the garage where prisoners were brought in. What struck me as so unusual was that some of the prisoners arrested would not cause any trouble until left alone with me.

As I have alluded to earlier, I had worked heavy construction with my father's business for ten years; swinging a 12LB. sledge hammer and throwing concrete into a dump truck. We would tear down a two-car garage in one day, and break up and load the garage floor and entire driveway the next day. This helped me build my muscles. Back to lock up…

I had three prisoners waiting, as I was completing the processing on one. When I gave him an ink pen to sign for his property, he raised his arm up and tried to stab me in the chest! I caught his wrist as he thrust downward, slid my hand over his clenched fist and smashed the ink pen to pieces. As his eyes widened in surprise, I struck him with a devastating right hook. He crumpled to the floor like he had been shot. He was out cold! As he laid there I said, "Next," to a shocked prisoner. "Just step over him," I gestured.

There was a large steel door across from the processing table. It led to a large concrete room called the bull pen, where there were stationary benches along the walls. After processing two prisoners, I told them to carry my assailant into the holding area.

That winter I was reassigned to the Doorman's job for the day. I thought everything was going well. Two officers brought a prisoner into lock up. They said he had taken his belt off and was beating school children. At that moment, he seemed quiet and unassuming.

When the prisoner processing was completed, I took him back to the main lock up. I had four or five prisoners in that section. I put him in a cell across from them and went to the lobby. I usually got along well with the prisoners; today was no exception.

Within a few minutes, I thought I heard a commotion. I went back to lock up and the prisoners across from the new one were yelling. It seems that the one I had just locked up was spitting on them through the cell bars!

Unlocking his door, I said. "Alright, come on out of there!"

I took him around the corner to the end of the cat walk. It was the last cell where there were no other prisoners. I ordered him into the open cell door. As he was going in, he stopped in the doorway, turned around and grabbed a cell bar on either side of the doorway. Using them as leverage, he pulled his body forward knocking me into the cell behind me. By surprise, he hit me with a sucker punch. Just that quick I was on my back.

He jumped on me and tried to choke me, "Call your police buddies now," he smirked. I looked at the back of my right hand. It was cut and bleeding. I saw red for the first time in my life on me. My mind racing, I realized it was him or me. I'm sure that I received an adrenaline overdose.

From a prone position, I hit him with a punch so hard he stood up and fell against the wall backwards. I was on him before he could make a move. I never felt so strong, as I hit him with three more punches to the body. Subdued, he crumpled to the floor.

When I drug him back around the corner, the other prisoners were yelling to see if I was okay. They were in total shock, when I finally drug him into their view. We were both covered in his blood!

Other inmates offered to hold the combative prisoner while I went for help. In doing so, they would merely have had to stick their arms through the bars and hold the prisoners while I went for help. I allowed them to do so. Keep in mind that I was a rookie officer at that time.

As I left I told him, "See, I didn't need my police buddies!"

The officers were horrified, when they saw all of the blood on my uniform. They all came running behind me asking if I was alright.

The other officers and I arrived back to the cell block where the combative prisoner was being held by the other inmates. Unfortunately, when the prisonor was released, he rammed me in the stomach with his head. I went into another rage and began a relentless defense.

One sergeant made the mistake of trying to stop me. I inadvertently knocked him back violently.

One of the older prisoners began to talk to me very calmly saying, "We helped you. Now you're wrong, young man!"

It was like someone had put brakes on me. I looked at the old timer and let the prisoner drop to the floor.

As my coworkers put him in another cell, I walked outside with no coat in the dead of a near zero night trying to come down from the fight or flight survival instinct. My lungs felt as if they were on fire, as I inhaled the subzero cooling oxygen. With more and more anger escaping with the exhaust of every breath, I could not feel the cold for some time.

Finally, I went back into the warmth of the lobby. Some of my co-workers were returning from the cell block when I entered. They told me that my prisoner was going wild in the cell. The next day it was discovered that he was mentally challenged.

Later in the week, because of my encounter, it was mandated city-wide that from then on any psych prisoner will be transferred straight to the Crisis Center at DGH. That mandate still holds true today.

By the way, it was a very long time before I had the Doorman's assignment again!

28 Chapter

THE GOLDEN RULE DRUNK

On another occasion, while working the street, my partner and I got a run to a disturbance and possible fight. (Keep in mind no run is ever routine.) We arrived at a boarding house type situation where there was basically a room full of beds. The caretaker approached us very upset. He told us this one tenant was drunk and got into an altercation with another. The intoxicated tenant had overturned beds and thrown other tenants around. He pointed the tenant out sitting on a bed.

We approached the man and told him we wanted to talk to him outside of the room. He said okay and came towards us.

We noticed he was no ordinary drunk. He had massive shoulders and arms, not to mention extraordinarily huge hands! Another thing I noticed right away was his wrists were bigger than my ankles, and our cuffs would not fit over them. I told him to stand still while I talked to my partner.

"Did you see what I saw?" I said. My partner immediately got on the prep and called for another car. To our dismay, there were no cars available. We were on our own, and this was one of those situations where you must think your way out of danger.

I told my partner, "You drive while I do the talking. Head for the station very cautiously."

Then I told the man who was about ten years older than me, around his early thirties, "How would you like to hang out with me and my partner; our ride is just outside?"

To my surprise he said, "Okay, let's go."

We got in the scout car and slowly started for the station. He was still intoxicated and physically dangerous. However, as we rode, he became even more friendly. He said, "Hey, I like you fellas. Pull into that gas station. I wanna buy you some gas!"

I told him, "Thank you very much, but we have a full tank."

He said, "Okay. Are you hungry?"

We answered, "No, thank you."

He continued, "You know, I like you guys. You are alright with me!"

"We're glad!" was our response.

Finally, we made it to the station and pulled into the garage near the prisoner's door. We said to the prisoner, "We would like for you to be our guest. Come on in."

We were truly surprised when he said, "Okay, I don't mind. I like you policemen!"

As we walked into the prisoner processing area, we told the Doorman that we would process this one. Then we got started taking his property for safe keeping.

One of the prisoners in the bull pen started blurting out insults. "Hey, you," he said to our prisoner, "Don't trust those no good cops. They're going to steal your money!"

"Shut up. These are my friends!" Our prisoner said to the trouble maker.

"If they are your friends, why are they locking you up?"

Our prisoner responded, "You don't see any handcuffs on me, and if you don't shut up, I'll take care of you!"

I couldn't help but to do a little instigating. "I see he is not going to leave us alone. Would you like for us to let you in there so you can have a talk with him?"

He said, "Hell, yes. He can't talk to my friends that way!"

I looked at my partner. He smiled and let our new pal in the bull pen. There was an instant commotion. We could hear the heckler screaming through the heavy steel door.

After a couple of minutes, we opened the door and saw the heckler knocked out on the floor. The other prisoners were huddled against the wall in fear, and our prisoner was lying on one of the wall benches sound asleep! We charged him as a Golden Rule Drunk and let him go at dawn that morning. One of our better shifts!

Chapter 29

HERE'S TO THE BLUE KNIGHTS OF THE "D"

The State of Michigan does not have capital punishment, (the death penalty) as most of you know. It does, however, require the utmost training of its officers: class room instruction, as well as familiarization with hand guns, long guns, not to mention firearms qualifications.

In the academy, this training is repeated over, and over, and OVER! The city, state, and federal laws concerning when to shoot are constantly changing, and every six months we are reinstructed and tested. There is no room for error or failure; as many defense attorneys are just waiting to pounce on you. I hate to say it, but simply for monetary gain.

I don't have to tell you about the added pressure from the department's scrutiny of your actions, while in the performance of your duty. That is why state law, criminal law, federal law, court procedure, arrest warrants, city ordinance, and much more are crammed into your heads. This is because in a state with no capital punishment you have the power over life and death during your performance in the line of duty. These decisions you must make in a split second, in the face of death, will be with you forever. To face this everyday deadly threat, you must rely on your training, constant practice and, I reiterate, situational awareness.

I desperately hope that this writing is received with the best of intentions and can serve as an eye opener for our good citizens, as well as a training manual for all of my brother and sister officers everywhere. Nothing would please me more than to know I kept you and yours out of harms' way. Just think, a literary way to save lives, even after 10 years of retirement!

Like I alluded to earlier, even in retirement there is no such thing as an ex-police officer. We still retain the same mental vigor, passion, knowhow, and combat tactics as when we were spanking new rookies. To see crimes and injustice still pains us deeply, however, we can still help. You know where to find us. Ask around. Come to a union meeting or retirement party. Meet us at a shooting range to see some real shooting. Just bring your patience and respect, and a whole world of street experience awaits you. I never lived, fought, partied, or preyed on predators with finer professionals than my DPD Crew. Here's to all of those that maintained their honor for their brother and sister officers, even in the face of temptation or weakness. To me, you are the Seed of Magnificent Courage; and I Salute the Sacrifice you have made for an Ideal! Here's to you, living or departed. Here's to The Blue Knights of the "D." True heroes. From An American Crime fighter. I salute your sacrifice!

30 Chapter

ARE WE REALLY MEAN?

Many times, while riding through the most dangerous areas of the streets, I could sense the hate and, after many attacks, even I felt the fear. However, this feeling could not stop me from returning to meet this haunting danger time and time again.

I began to realize that fear itself is the enemy and to overcome it I must become the threat by way of pure intellect and split-second thinking. One of my plans was to sharpen my skills from each dangerous encounter, in order that my partner and I should survive. We came to realize that when we were in hunting mode, our prey was a most dangerous game. MAN!!

Unfortunately, the only thing they would respect was a pure violent overwhelming, sometimes deadly force. In the underground, and in the black market, our adversaries are able to obtain an array of weapons to use against us. For our breed, this is a continuous threat and will be forever present in our chosen profession.

Some people ask why police officers are so mean. We are not all mean. Please know that it takes pure dedication and a love of humanity in order for us to know when to control the physical aggression.

Regrettably, as I sit here and write for you, there has been another police-related shooting. This situation, however, will result in the officer, caught on film, possibly being indicted for murder. Here again, this kind of deadly force over a misdemeanor traffic stop can damage our image; not to mention put us at further risk.

To help resolve most of these situations where officers feel so threatened, I encourage these police departments to man your cruisers with at least two officers. There is absolutely no excuse for hatred of any kind: race, creed, ethnic origin, or religion, on any police department, for we are charged to serve and protect. There is no getting away from our sworn oath of office, remember?

This profession is wrought with enough danger, personal injury, loss of life, and hardship to last a lifetime. As we always respond to your emergency calls, and you are gratified to see us coming to the rescue, let us not fail to save the day. Please understand this, if we, on the other hand, are in trouble and need your help, don't hesitate to rise to the occasion so that we may live to respond another day. Nothing feels more rewarding than knowing that citizens appreciate us for the tremendous danger we encounter to keep you safe. Knowing this, makes the average officer want to move heaven and earth for you. Sometimes even beyond our shift, if necessary.

31 Chapter

POLICE OFFICERS AS VICTIMS

You may never think about it, however, your very own police officers are sometimes victims of crimes. When I joined The Force, one of the protocols was you had to live in the city.

My first encounter as a victim occurred while I was visiting a female friend. Someone stole my new vehicle. It was recovered the next day, not very far away, sitting on blocks and wheels gone. This occurred in my precinct. I was shocked.

About 15 years later, my family and I were the victims of a B&E of our home, set up by my next door neighbor's son who dropped out of school to feed his drug habit. I knew my neighbor's son was the planner and look out, because they broke in on his side of my home. They only got a few items, leaving behind numerous electronic devices. I knew they would be back. The same day as the break in I had the home armed with heavy steel doors and bars on the windows where they had gained entry.

Exactly two weeks later, under the surveillance of my doped up neighbor, watching as my wife and I went out to dinner, his crew returned. What they did not realize was that there were two adult baby sitters inside with my children.

Their plan was like something out of rocket science, or so they thought.

They drove up in their own vehicle and got out to break into my van, which was parked in front of our home. They had planned to use my van to haul the stolen items. While this was in progress, several other thieves stormed the front porch with a small log type piece of wood to ram the door.

Before they could make a move, my youngest son opened the door curtains, thinking we were returning home.

The punks leaped off of the porch, screaming a warning to the ones in my van and the driver of the vehicle.

Unknown to the lead rocket scientist, my son got a good look at him. Not more than a month later he was out front playing. He ran into the house and told me the perp was standing on the corner, a half block away. I had my wife call for back up, as I strapped on my 44 mag.

When I approached the corner, there were about six teens standing in the driveway. I told them all not to move and that they were under suspicion for B&E.

One very large teen, about five inches taller than my 6'3" said, "How you gonna stop us?"

Stalling for time, which seemed like an eternity, I said, "I am not alone. I brought six friends with me!"

Putting my hand inside my coat, I grabbed the handle of my gun. Feeling certain of death, I stared him down, unflinching. Everyone froze.

At that point, four scout cars came sliding up, wheels locked and squealing. Before they could get out, three more thieves came out of nowhere. I pulled my badge out, and the police crew pounced on everyone around me. I pointed out the ones I wanted detained.

My family was a little frightened, because my young son was the key witness. He had seen them on the porch and again on the street.

To make a long story shorter, the sly defense attorney repeatedly set up future court dates. Three times we showed up only to be sent home. I knew what the lawyer knew; if we had missed one court date, he could get the case thrown out. We never missed or came late. I overheard the lawyer tell the punk, "You might as well plead guilty. No judge or jury will go against the child's testimony." And so it went. The rocket science gang was busted up.

Later, I told my neighbor that I knew his son had set my home up and he was the look out. I also told him that if I caught his son on my property again, well let's just say, he would be a look out in another world.

It would be about three years later when my son and his cousins were playing in front of my garage. I was on leave and was about to relax. Unknown to me, several days earlier, a friend of my nemesis had gotten into a physical confrontation with some other teens. The nemesis had talked another friend into bringing his father's AK47 to the angry teen's home just several houses away from my own.

My next door neighbor was always at work, when his dropout son was up to no good. The son took the weapon onto the upstairs back porch to practice. Mind you, this was a summer day in a very nice neighborhood. There was a young father that just happened to be in his back yard directly across from this porch.

My neighbor's son looked the young father in the eye, aimed the assault weapon in the air and shot off some 20 rounds or more.

Women and children were running and screaming.

When I came running out of the house, my son and his cousin pointed out who it was that fired the shots.

I went inside and called for backup, grabbed my weapon, and ran toward the location. As I approached, I met an off duty sergeant still in uniform and said, "I think the shot came from this house!"

We walked the length of the driveway into the backyard and spotted numerous shell casings in the grass directly below the upstairs porch. That's when we observed three teen males exiting the side driveway door. One of them was my neighbor's son carrying a black plastic bag. We pointed our weapons toward the suspects and shouted, "Freeze; don't move." However, they ignored our warning and proceeded to enter a vehicle parked in the driveway.

The sergeant and I moved quickly to the vehicle, ordered the youths to surrender, and forcefully took the black plastic bag. Upon further examination, we discovered the bag contained the AK-47, still hot from rapid fire and partially melting the plastic bag.

Just as we took possession of the weapon, multiple police cars surrounded the scene.

The sergeant and I gave the responding officers the weapon, the prisoners, and showed them the shell casing evidence. We prepared to follow them to the police station to make our Preliminary Complaint Report (P.C.R.).

Fast Forward to the Pretrial Exam...

The eye witness and I that looked the perp in the eye before he boldly pulled the trigger were for the prosecution. My neighbor and his son sat with the defense attorney. Proceedings started right away. The prosecutor made his case presenting the pure facts.

Now here comes the defense, "I want to question the officer who arrested my client." That was me. In full uniform and armed with a copy of my P.C.R. I had written on the day of the felony arrest, I was called to the stand and sworn in.

The defense attorney started out by asking me how many years I had been an officer. At that time, I told him about 21 years.

The defense lawyer immediately shouted, "You see, Your Honor, this officer has been on the police force long enough to know how to lie!"

The judge ordered, "We will dispense with these accusations, council. Do you have any pertinent questions for this officer?"

"Yes," he reiterated, "Why did you arrest my client in the first place, where, what date, and time?"

I addressed my attention to the judge, and asked if I may read from my report.

The defense attorney quickly interrupted, "Your Honor, I object to this officer reading from whoever wrote these notes!"

The judge turned to me, and asked, "Who wrote this report, officer?"

I responded, "These are my handwritten notes on an official Police Report, Your Honor." The judge noted, "So you wrote this report on an official police document, contained several copies, and submitted it through police channels, retaining a copy for yourself as evidence, with your handwritten signature to read before this court?"

I affirmed, "Yes sir, Your Honor!"

"I confirm that this handwritten document, sworn to by this officer, is deemed by this court as legal evidence in this court's proceedings. You may read your report, officer."

After I read my accurate report, the judge deemed the exam bound over for trial.

I felt my many years of professional experience rewarding. I told the only eye witness, "I will see you in court!"

Some weeks had passed, including the court date, and no response from the prosecutor. I called the prosecutor's office to inquire and was told the slick defense attorney had the case thrown out on some trumped up technicality!

Naturally, I asked, "What can I do? This was too serious to be thrown out." Thinking to myself, he had already gotten away with a B&E of my home.

The main prosecutor picked up the phone and told me if I came to his office, he would reissue the warrant. However, I would have to execute it and make the arrest all over again!

From the onset, I knew that the perp's father was already pissed off at me for arresting his dope head son. I had tried to explain to him that I could have shot him for not obeying my command to halt. This was to no avail. His emotions had overruled my logic.

In order to make this arrest, I knew I had to use cunning sophistication. I knew the father worked days without fail, and the son had dropped out of school to savor his drug habit. I waited for the perfect set of distractions. The opportunity quickly arose.

The felon was celebrating his exoneration by giving a party. As usual, his father was working hard. I knew that if I had to serve the warrant I might have to beat him and his crew into a coma.

The crooked defense attorney was right about one thing. With my two decades of experience, I had learned to be resourceful. So I knew there was another way. There was a 30 series (plainclothes, unmarked car) crew in the precinct where I lived that I was familiar with. Their undercover covert experience was just what the doctor ordered.

I had them come to my home undercover, of course, out of sight of the of the dope party. I gave them a synopsis of the situation and turned them loose. They called me about 30 minutes later and told me my warrant had been served. This happened after the perp had been tricked into giving his correct name, which was on the warrant. He put up a useless fight and was quickly overpowered and arrested again.

Unfortunately, his father got him out on bond, pending his felony trial.

Several days later, being the big time thug that he thought he was, this perp and his cohorts terrorized my family by ganging up in front of my home while I was away on my post. And, if that was not enough, he and his gang would sit on his front porch waiting for me to come home. "There he is. Get a good look at him!" the felon would exclaim.

By this time, I had upgraded to a Street Combat double action 45 cal. semi-automatic, which I pulled out in plain view every night for their edification.

This harassment continued for almost a month, with him trying to provoke me before his court date came up.

At his trial, the judge gave me an opportunity to give testimony on his conduct toward my family and myself. After his conviction, I made sure I went to his sentencing to give additional testimony about the threats my family and I endured awaiting trial.

His crooked attorney was speechless. It was his client's first offense. However, due to his callous disregard for the law and my family, the judge gave him the maximum sentence, without parole, not to mention the devastating testimony of my eye witness. The sentence came to 2 ½ years with two years' parole added on.

I thought this whole episode was over, until I received an order to report to Internal Affairs! I reported as ordered.

As I walked into their office, they seemed shocked.

"Officer reporting as ordered. Is there something wrong?"

One of the investigators came up to me and stated, "Now that you are here, we understand that your neighbor was sadly mistaken. He asked to be put in a room with you for two minutes! After seeing you in person, we now know, with your physical stature, he didn't stand a chance."

"What is this all about," I asked?

"Well, he stated that you pulled your gun on him."

I explained how his son and his thug friends waited for me to come home every night from work. Therefore, I took my gun out for protection, never aiming at no one, which is my lawful right as a sworn DPD officer."

The false complaint was dismissed before I could leave the office.

By the way, parole was explained to him the day he arrived home by the same 30 series crew. This was in addition to his 2-1/2-year prison term. I personally deemed this action necessary and poetic justice for his wanna be gangster attitude.

This was only a couple of the hardships my family went through living in the neighborhood where everyone knew me and pointed out, "That is where the cop lives!" No one ever pointed out where the riff-raft hung out, or what illegal activities they were up to. However, one of their biggest hair-brained schemes was conducting their criminal activities on the very block where I resided. This turned out to be a very costly error in judgment. Their one dimensional thinking blinded them to the fact that I had C.O.S. rank over the largest gang in the city, The DPD!!

Chapter 32

IT'S A FAMILY AFFAIR

There is no doubt that the life of a policeman is not peaches and cream. There was always the occasional stereotype family trouble runs with its inherent threats of hidden danger. Never knowing what to expect until all hell breaks loose, and then you and your partner are IT!

This scenario plays out a thousand times a day all over the U.S. We come because we are called. Someone in the household has either caused a disturbance, a misdemeanor, or a felony. We come because a neighbor may be afraid for their neighbor's safety. We come because the caller is under attack and may already be badly beaten. We come because a loved one calls and fears for the worst for you and or your children's lives. We come as fast as we can. Sometimes even when it is too late; a whole family gone at the hands of the father, mother, a child, B&E perps, or some other emotionally disturbed person. We come to help you, even when we know you hate us and will possibly try to kill us. It does not sound logical, because people are mentally or violently unpredictable and our uniform becomes the target of that rage.

A woman calls because her husband or boyfriend has beaten her senseless. We arrive in time to see him assault her again. We restrain the subject. The woman disappears and returns with a knife and tries to stab the officers. It takes one, or both of us, to be observant enough not to become a victim or statistic. Now we have two arrests. This scenario is not uncommon.

Another true incident: "18-4; we are receiving a family trouble run at this location."

"18-4 on the way, radio!"

As two Detroit policewomen respond, the caller is a battered woman. She waits at the door as they arrive. They all walk in the door, while the caller tells on her husband. The instant the husband spots the crew in the house, he bolts for the upstairs bedroom, a quick thinking officer on his heels. Just as he grabs a hand gun, the officer is on him, a struggle for life and death ensues. Alone, and with no way to radio for help, the officer subdues and disarms the felon. After cuffing the subject, she marches him downstairs under arrest. Another deadly situation has been averted without a death or becoming a statistic. You can chalk this up to a superbly trained officer and a fearless fighter for good. Yes, IT'S MY SISTER!!! Belinda Koss. One of the many fearless BLUE KNIGHTS IN THE "D"!!

Chapter 33

WELCOME ABOARD, POLICEWOMEN!

Following is an article from the Detroit Historical Society written by Chris Paris, and I quote:

"The Detroit Police Department embraced innovation and change in the late 19th and early 20th centuries. In 1893, L.T. Toliver became the city's first African-American police officer. That same year, Police Superintendent Morgan Collins hired Marie Owen, the first female officer in the United States.

The Detroit Police Department was one of the very first in the country to use automobiles for patrol. In 1922, the department became the first in the nation to use radio dispatch technology." I was the Class of 70 H: 70 for the year 1970 and H for our class group. There were approximately eighty-two males and one female. We were called Student Patrolmen and Patrolwomen. During this time, hiring qualifications consisted of a high school diploma for men, age twenty-one, minimum weight 147 pounds, minimum height 5'7" inches, and a clean record, no felonies. Requirements for women: a two year Associates Degree, clean record, minimum age twenty-one. Academic Qualifications: pass all spelling tests, criminal law, state law, city ordinances, firearms handling and training, shooting qualifications, hand combat, crowd control, and arrest procedures. Our female students had the same requirements, except for the physical training (P.T.).

We were required to pass all of these studies and activities. Fail any one of these categories and you will have failed the entire course. There was one alternative: fall back to the next class and start over. The men's final test was to run a three-mile course, No exceptions.

Upon graduation, the men were assigned to all of the precincts throughout the city. The women were assigned to W.D. (Women's Division), 7th floor of the police headquarters, 1300 Beaubien St. They wore plain clothes.

The W.D. was established in 1920. They were armed with 38 caliber revolvers. Their assignment: rape investigations, child neglect, juvenile delinquency, female abuse, and checking businesses for illegal minors.

In 1976, an outgoing Chief of Police, who was in disfavor of the mayor, banished all previous qualifications for males and females; physical, age, gender, and education for women. This meant that there was no longer a height, weight, age, strength, or two year Associates Degree component for academic entry. This meant that for the first time in Detroit police history, policewomen graduated in 1974 to all precincts and plainclothes assignments just as the men; full street duty.

When I learned of this complete reversal of department policy I thought of my sister. I gave her heads up information. Following my instructions, she went to the recruiting office and applied. She was given the written test right away and passed. She then passed the physical agility and oral board, which was crucial, just as I had done years earlier.

The oral board consisted of several seasoned plainclothes officers. She was subjected to a barrage of police-related situations. Her response to these questions determined whether she was considered police material and passed on to the academy. My sister passed this verbal test with flying colors. Needless to say, but I will, I am proud of her.

There was one more step: a visit from two plainclothes investigators to the home without appointment for job placement with the department. However, her husband was the only one home when the plainclothes team arrived. He let them know that neither they nor the Detroit police were welcome in his home.

Having accumulated a great deal of experience concerning departmental police procedures, I advised my sister that she need only to pick up where she left off. She contacted recruiting and set an appointment for the investigators' return. This time she was the only one home. From this point on, everything progressed rapidly. She found herself in the Police Academy in no time.

The year was now 1977. My family and I moved in with my sister and her family. This timely move made it possible for my sister to attend her academic classes, while my wife, at that time, took good care of my sister's children.

Meanwhile, the relationship between my sister and her husband became severely strained, as he had become almost insanely jealous. My sister, however, was fortunately able to concentrate on her studies. In a little over three months, she was able to graduate a brand new officer.

Soon after, we all moved out. She moved in with our parents and immediately filed for divorce. Even as a single parent, she continued to excel amongst her peers. With constant and extreme street input from her big brother, she became a shining example of Detroit's finest. Her on-duty street exploits boarded on legend; Again, I'm proud to convey.

At the height of recruitment, hiring the D.P.D.'s female officers outnumbered all of the female police in all of the police departments in the United States. Sadly, even as I write this on Wednesday, May 19, 2015, it has come to my attention that we have lost a sister officer; ambushed trying to serve a warrant. She was a new mom. It cost her life to put down a criminal that should never have been born. This is my personal feeling. I am grateful that I was off the mean streets before I started my family. Therefore, they didn't experience the heartbreak and sorrow of losing a loved one the way many officers' families have.

In late 1969, when I first applied for DPD, I was so excited about the idea that I never mentioned it to my parents. When I turned 18, it was mandatory to report to the induction center. This was a physical and a written test to qualify for enlistment into the military.

Unknown to me, my parents had prepared for such an event with an attorney. I found out years later from my parents, as an only son, I could not and would not qualify for the armed services. Later, after I qualified and was accepted onto the police force, I could not know the shock and fear they must have felt.

My father was calm and simply stated, "Don't get yourself killed." My mother never expressed her fears directly to me. However, she was quite vocal to my dad. From time to time he would pull me to the side and inform me how much my street duty worried my mom. I loved working the street so much. I took the warning with a grain of salt. That was until my partner was killed, whom my mother knew and was a family friend. That day was the first time I ever saw my mother cry. I was in a state of shock that changed my way of thinking about my mother's worry and her feelings. A few years later, I relented and transferred to C.O.S. (Communications Operation Section) dispatch.

Chapter 34

THERE'S NO ROOM FOR RACISM

It was a typical summer night in the city around dusk. My partner and I spotted a wanted subject on Woodward, a main street dividing the city of Detroit between east and west.

The subject broke for a side street and ran on a porch. We were in hot pursuit, leaving the scout car doors open as we chased him into the house. The male ran up three flights of stairs past numerous family members who stood frozen in shock at the sight the police running through their house. After a brief struggle, we apprehended him on the third floor.

As we attempted to leave, the family blocked our path. We instinctively pulled our weapons. In the heat of the chase, we forgot we had radioed our position when we ran into the house.

Standing there in a stale mate, we could hear numerous police cars arriving. Our scout car marked our point of entry. As our back up made their way up the stairs, we could hear a disturbance during the arrest of those that attempted resistance. It was music to our ears and an incredibly refreshing release of tension not to have to kill or be killed.

As we exited the house, we witnessed a sea of scout cars and a crowd of curious, but peaceful, citizens. We conveyed our arrest without further incident.

It is a national pastime watching the police and firemen in action, whether you hate them or not. There are the curious, the fans, the accusers, and sometimes the hecklers. The latter two usually try to incite the crowd to violence. This is especially true if the police crews are not racially mixed. This type of danger takes the finesse of a racially diverse police force, which has been typically demonstrated in the DPD, which has placed us as the number one city for non- racial police involved killings in America. The lesson we have learned is that it takes a police force that resembles the citizens it is sworn to serve. This is a lesson that must be demonstrated throughout our racially-challenged cities. Without this type of compliance, sensitivity training for certain officers is like putting a band aid on a severe wound. In other words, there is going to be a long hot summer, even into the winter. Reaction to police-related murders will erupt into violent unrest and the return of an old evil for innocent police officers.

In my opinion, our communities cannot sustain an evil for an evil. It is our task to police ourselves and weed out those who slipped through the cracks, who care nothing of human life when that person doesn't resemble them.

We must also stop these types who are once fired to being hired by another department, which is what resulted in a child's killing. Either they ignored or failed to challenge his prior questionable record or dismissal.

For a true crime fighter, there can be no room for an ethnic or racially motivated shooting. This is not and will not be a part of our blue blood integrity or Brotherhood. In my heart, I know this to be the truth for the majority of my sworn associates. This poisonous venom within our midst must be eradicated before it can spread any further. So far it seems the only catalyst toward change is the exposure coming from these incidents being caught on camera. Whenever one of these ill-fated loses of life occurs, unfortunately, it tarnishes all of our badges.

As I write these very words, here in April of 2015, there have been two more killings and a high profile beating by officers on a traffic stop earlier last month.

35 Chapter

YOUNG INNOCENTS

Another of our crew received a run to investigate a flat. Upon arrival, they probed what seemed to be an empty dwelling and a child walked in. She was about 10 or 11 and relayed an unbelievable story. The parents had just up and left several weeks ago, taking the furniture and leaving the children behind with no explanation and no warning.

She went on to explain that she had a sister and brother. Holding a bag, she took them to a closet door. When she opened the door, there huddled together were two small, frightened children, ages 2 and 4, sitting alone in the dark, where their big sister had told them to wait for her. The bag in her hand was food she had saved from her school lunch. Everyday she would come home at lunchtime with the food for the youngsters. This is what they were living on.

This event is not unusual to us. It's the situations that are different. Being so young and innocent, these children seem to be more responsible than their no account parents.

As always, they were taken straight to the precinct station where the officers chipped in to feed and comfort them until representatives from Social Services arrived. Then they are taken to a foster home.

Sometime later, my partner and I received a run where a concerned neighbor had called about children left home alone. It was winter. We pulled up to the scene of the house. At the time, we did not detect any activity. We knocked and a child of about 11 years of age answered the door. She was holding an infant. Our first question naturally was, "Are your parents home?"

She responded, "No. My mother is not home."

We walked toward the kitchen and asked, "Are you the oldest child?

"Yes," she answered.

Once in the kitchen, I opened the refrigerator door and found two large beer bottles, one empty and the other almost empty.

As I walked into the living room, I was shocked to see my partner surrounded by nine other children. In total, there were 11, all a year apart!

We asked the 11-year-old where her mother was. She didn't know. She had left a while ago!

Just then we heard a noise in the kitchen. When we returned to the kitchen where the noise came from, we saw three large rats running across the top of the stove! We had seen enough and notified Radio to send several scout cars.

We told the oldest child to put as many clothes as she could find on the little ones. The scout cars arrived promptly.

While we readied the children, the oldest brought a box to us. The box was full of newborn puppies!

I said, "Okay, bring them along as well."

We filled all three scout cars and headed for the station.

The desk supervisor was overwhelmed. He asked, "What's going on!"

We said we couldn't leave them, as we took up a collection to feed them right away. We pleaded with Social Services to try to keep them together, and wrote our report to take them away from the unknown mother.

Another devastating and heart-wrenching occasion occurred in the dead winter. While on patrol, we received a Radio Run to see what's wrong at such and such location.

Upon arrival, we were permitted entry by a very young male. When we entered an upstairs flat, there was another young male and a young female sitting together. The male that met us at the door showed us a baby crib. In the crib, was an infant male lying motionless! As my partner checked the infant, I asked the male what happened.

With a smile on his face he stated, "The baby would not stop crying!"

My partner looked at me and gave me our signal which meant the infant was deceased.

I asked the youth who he was.

He responded, "The baby's father."

I read him his rights.

He reacted by saying, "All I did was stop him from crying," still smiling.

Just then, a young girl came in barely dressed for winter.

We found out she was the baby's mother and had gone for milk.

She walked to the crib, as my partner hugged her and told her the news.

She went hysterical. "All I did was go for milk. He was okay when I left!"

The father was still smiling. When I took him down, he tried to put up a fight. As I said, he tried.

Just when I was using sufficient force to make the arrest, the sergeant walked in. He pulled me off the baby killer.

I explained what had taken place and then he took over. After a brief moment, I had to pull him off!

We called for EMS, then Homicide Detectives, and finally the medical examiner from the morgue. We held all present for Homicide: the so-called father, his two friends as witnesses, and the young mother who was being treated by medics.

This was my first infant homicide, and this was one too many. The incidents of abused children are a long one, unfortunately, and I personally believe that some people should not be allowed to have such wonderful little angels.

As concerned human beings, we learned how to use some of that power invested in us by the people of the City of Detroit and the State of Michigan. Whenever we found a flagrant breach of child abuse, we did not pass the buck. If the abusive parents were around, they were instantly arrested. We physically took possession of the little victims. Once at the station, we took care of the children's immediate needs and wrote an airtight police report that no underhanded defense could wiggle out of.

For the safety of those innocents, we saw this as our duty and that is what we do. It is the disciplined nature of a police officer to be cotton soft with innocents on one hand and be devastatingly aggressive with killers and other life-threatening felons on the other hand; and to know the difference between them. We have to measure their every threat with a higher physical force and know how not to overreact. To pull off this balancing act takes one hell of police officer who can learn from the best senior officers.

There is a very thin line between life and death and an even shorter time span, less than a split second. I have seen this tragedy, however, my eyes were left in denial at the instant reality of certain death.

Chapter 36

ONE-PERCENT IS NOT THE MAJORITY

On any given day or night, even when things seem to be calm, you never know until you hear that dreaded "Officer-in-Trouble" run and what might happen. You have been trained, however, by your seniors to make that run no matter what.

Alright, readers: hop in, if you dare, and let's go to the most dangerous run a police crew can make.

Keep in mind this call does not have to be in your precinct. It can occur in the opposite ends of the city and rarely in another city. Still there is no distinction as to the dire straits or the necessity to get there at almost no cost.

When you and your partner are the ones calling for help, believe you me, it seems like an eternity before help arrives. Here is where you separate the men from the boys, so to speak. No matter how fast you drive, or how fast you can arrive, if you crack up, or blow an engine, you are out of the lifesaving business!

Imagine the feeling of being dead in the water, your car out of service, as you hear your fellow officers responding at a high rate of speed and saving the day. This is another lesson in how critical it is to know every aspect of your cruiser's performance and how to negotiate through high traffic intersections, while maintaining a good high speed pace, safely.

If you have accepted the challenge to ride with us, by now your heart is probably in your throat, as we negotiate near miss accidents with citizens' vehicles that usually fail to yield for our life and death emergencies. Slamming on the brakes, flooring the gas with precision, the police siren is almost deafening, as you are thrown from side to side, front to back, coupled with the adrenaline rush pulsating through your veins. It is an exciting danger you won't soon forget. Mind you, all this has taken place before you even arrive at the call for help. You must be ready for a gunfight. Ready to run into a hail of gunfire, a violent hostile crowd, possible injured officers, total confusion, attacks from every direction, and/or being completely surrounded. All of these scenes racing through your mind, because you have seen it all before.

Finally, at the scene, you observe a crowd and a handful of officers in a fight for their lives. As the backup officers bail out of the cruiser to assist their fellow policemen and policewomen, you are frozen in astonishment at the level of violence you have never witnessed before. Meanwhile, more and more scout cars arrive.

Finally, everything is under control and the injured and the incarcerated are conveyed from the scene. Your crew has made an arrest, therefore, you will have to ride back with a supervisor. Thankfully, this was not a deadly shooting or cutting scene, but the day is just beginning and this was only one run. Now you must prepare your mental and physical condition for the unknown. This is the non-stop life of a street officer in a sprawling urban city like The "D."

Okay, come on, reader, let's grab a coffee while we have a chance. Hop in. Let's go!

The police report from the "Officer-in-Trouble" run and arrest have taken several hours. The shift is almost over.

Look! A vehicle has just run a stop sign right in front of us. Let's pull him over.

A traffic stop is a different animal and has just put you in another realm of the unknown; and the unknown represents pure danger.

If you have time, write down the plate number and description of the vehicle, or call in the info. However, be in control of every aspect of this investigation. Be on guard for any abrupt or aggressive movements from the occupants. Treat this situation as though you and your partner's life depended on your every move. One day it will!

All of a sudden the vehicle speeds off. Instantly, your partner is on the radio announcing a chase, giving description, location and direction of the fleeing vehicle. Usually, with no regard for traffic conditions, the fleeing felon blows through red lights, drives against traffic, and accelerates too fast for safety.

About this time, the dispatcher comes back with info from the plate, the vehicle and possible occupants who are wanted for robbery and felony firearms warrants. This is a game changer! Strap in even tighter reader, because here we go again.

With the experience of high speed pursuit, your partner navigates the cruiser patiently and with precision, knowing that other scout cars are closing in on your position. The fleeing felons are becoming more and more desperate, as they cannot lose the closing scout car.

The officer behind the wheel knows he has to make a tactical move, sooner than later, thinking of a way to safely take out the vehicle and get in a safe place.

Knowing the area, and that there is a dead end street coming up, I move up to the driver's side and force him to make a hard right turn.

As he slams on the brakes, we are on them with guns drawn. More police cars are arriving. There is no escape. Suspects are in custody.

I am deeply saddened to write that three more officers have been fatally ambushed: one in New York and two in Hattiesburg, Mississippi.

The month of May 2015 has barely begun. Police officers are now under more scrutiny than any other time in history. The shooting of unarmed black males by white officers has really put us under the microscope. This has caused a feeling of mistrust that must not exist between the police and citizenry. Remember the 99% that you depend upon and trust to protect you with our very lives. Don't judge our dedication to serve and protect by the 1%.

37 Chapter

ANIMAL CRUELTY

Among the many officers I have been associated with, we all had this one thing in common: the love of animals. Yes, cruelty to animals is one of my pet peeves. I do harbor the feeling that those who harm and kill defenseless animals and pets eventually become killers of humans. Fighting dogs is one of the most atrocious of all. Just imagine a dog having no choice but to fight for its life, not having known any kindness or decency, just a constant regiment of hardcore physical training and abuse. What can be worse than this? I'll tell you, the violent life and death contest itself. Can it get any worse? Yes, for the loser! If he or she survives and is still able to fight, the horror continues. However, if the loser has life threatening injuries, it is either destroyed or left to die. This is unacceptable. Therefore, whenever we became aware of or received such a run, it was especially a high priority with me.

All of the participants, as well as the promoters and the trainers and owners of the animals, and the animal victims are all taken into custody. The animals were conveyed to the shelter for first aid and rehabilitation. If they were too far gone, they were put to sleep. Even this was more humane than their previous existence. I have no pity, only contempt, for the lowlife's who dared make a living from this form of animal torture and cruelty. I cannot express for you the pain I feel for these innocent creatures that do not have the capacity to understand WHY.

What is harder to fathom is how these perpetrators have no humane feelings or remorse for these victims that they created; only hate and anger for the losers that cost them money.

For myself, I could not be more diametrically opposed to these types, or any other violent career criminals who perpetuate their violence on the weak.

For some reason, I have always felt physically and mentally stronger when I was in a fight against evil. In those moments, I knew I could not be defeated. It is a righteous feeling!

38 Chapter

TIPPING THE SCALES OF JUSTICE

The FBI reports that the beginning of 2017 already shows a dangerous increase in police murders. And I repeat: only the best of us are being ambushed. What is the thinking, or lack thereof, to murder any officer? There is no escape. They will be caught or killed.

Let us add another dimension to this equation. Try this on for size. Have the criminals wear a certain uniform all the same with the words criminal across the chest. You can even arm them. Now, let us put all of the police officers in plain clothes and arm them also with any type of murderous weapon they choose: Teflon, hollow points, tracers, and any other so-called cop killer ammo, swords, machetes, knives, hatchets. Now, put the criminals on patrol out in the open throughout the neighborhoods, and have the police ambush the criminals with no warning or remorse. Have them celebrate and promote more killings to prove their manhood. Not very humane is it? Does not go over very well, does it? It would make a normal person sick to their stomach.

Here again, even as I write on Saturday, May 23rd, a young father learned of a personal protection order his estranged wife had issued against him. He took his family hostage. Shortly thereafter, he released all of the hostages except the wife. Hours later, the husband came out shooting.

Even though the Detroit police officers were in a defensive posture, the gunman's first shot struck an officer. The police returned fire, fatally wounding the assailant.

It seems as though I will not be able to complete my true story without reporting these never-ending fatal urban tragedies. Let's face it, "You do not get to be old by being a fool." That is a fact. Since I have escaped death in so many encounters, like so many other lawmen and women before me, I have lived to hold life as a very precious gift. However, there are still those who feel just the opposite. That is the equation and remains the number one threat to us and our community. Could it be for the criminals, as it is for the police, that when you are confronted by constant violence, you become one within its world? There is one difference; however, the police commit it to stop it. The criminals, on the other hand, use it as a weapon against anyone weaker and in a defenseless position, even unsuspecting officers.

So, how do we tip the scales of justice in favor of the defenseless and the weak who obey the laws and seek only to be happy and to live and let live?

There is a solution. However, it lies with our senior officers training our young officers.

I realized that some police officers had their weaknesses and they needed protecting also, like having a big brother. I remember some senior officers that had taken me under their wings when I was green. Therefore, when my time came, after about two years, I took the reins with intelligence prowess and the knowledge I had gained questioning and listening to the old timers who were a part of the greatest generation, World War Two Veterans. The advice I was given saved my life on more than one occasion. And now that life-saving information is still being passed on by me whenever I encounter a new officer willing to learn. This has taught me that these life-saving methods are perpetual.

Chapter 39

THE DISENFRANCHISED

Due to mental challenges, there are those that had the Lafayette Clinic to fall back on. There they received professional care and had a place to stay while being cared for. The DPD had the task of conveying the most violent patients to the old Detroit General Hospital. This was a daunting and dangerous police responsibility. Taking these citizens into custody, usually by force, was a physical struggle to say the least.

The most responsible task of these police runs was to restrain and convey these subjects without harming them. Unfortunately, in the most extreme circumstances, it was the officers that were injured.

In case you are asking how? Get in the scout car, because here comes a police run to answer your question.

"13-4 and all cars in the 13th precinct, we're getting a call for assistance at such and such address; a violent mental patient; the big auto (large prisoner truck) is at the scene."

As we arrive, you can see numerous police officers wrestling with a 6'-6" male throwing police in the air while they are trying to get him in the big auto. As we exit the scout car, we learn that some officers are down (a term meaning injured and out of action or terminal).

We know that we are in hot water, as we join in on the action. We decide the only thing to do is have several officers rush the group forcing everyone to fall into the truck.

At this point, one officer slams the door shut and the driver is told to head for DGH.

I'm afraid you riding with me will have to get another ride. As the driver heads for the Crisis Center, we are all inside the truck still wrestling with this large man who seems to have super human strength.

The driver notifies Dispatch to call the DRH Crisis Center and inform them we are on the way with an uncontrolled violent mental. The DRH Crisis Center is the only hospital that would take psych patients.

There was a resourceful assistant waiting at the dock, which was the emergency entrance, with a heavy rope. As the big auto backed up to the dock, the driver had us hold the struggling man against a steel beam while he ran around him with the rope. A nurse gave him a sedative in the arm, and soon he was unable to move. Now it was time to attend to the wounded officers, as they were being conveyed to the same hospital.

It was well known in those days, and even now as I write this, that all serious traumas, especially gunshot wounds, were conveyed to DGH. If you could be saved, their E.R. had the best surgical team. The hospital is now call Detroit Receiving Hospital (D.R.H.) and still has the best Trauma Team.

Back in my day on the streets, I saw a team remove a round from a man's heart while it was still beating and spurting blood! It was one of the most amazing sights I have ever witnessed and, believe me, I have seen quite a few, including an innocent man walking down the street and suddenly being shot in the chest with an arrow.

Getting back to the disenfranchised…

In the early-to mid-1970s, with no warning, the governor decided to close the Lafayette Clinic. This executive decision displaced all of the stricken citizens with nowhere to go.

This political action placed the burden of responsibility mainly on the DPD, who had to respond to all of these types of police runs. The Detroit Receiving Hospital, Emergency Crisis Center, could only take those psych patients who were violent or dangerous to themselves. The Lafayette Clinic was never reopened, and the fallout from that callous political favor still impacts the city to this very day; with so many of our homeless a part of that closure.

It has been over forty years since this occurrence and no resolution to this travesty has occurred. The DPD is still responding to any and all of these calls and making conveyances to DRH who can only treat these victims for so many days only to be released back on the streets. At what cost and to whose profit? We can only ponder.

What is it that stops some of us from allowing others to love, live life, and enjoy the freedom and liberty to do so and be safe in ours the greatest Nation on Earth? Yet, who am I to ask? Only a retired police officer for life, still doing what I can for those who can't do for themselves; which I believe is The American Way!

I feel truly blessed at my age to still be a formidable physical presence in the face of evil and or wrong doers. I fervently hope that the coming generation can protect my generation in our old age, as we have protected their ancestors in their time of need. As I see it, no one starts out in life with the goal to become a failure, or homeless, yet there are still those in our society who take pleasure in looking down on the have nots.

40 Chapter
THE GIFT

As a certified lawman or lawwoman, you have been given a license to kill by the authority of the city, state, and federal government. We are trained to direct our fire on a target for maximum effect.

I have been quizzed by citizens for years asking, "Why don't you shoot the bad guys in the arm or leg?" Sounds like a seriously legitimate question, and they were serious when they asked. However, shooting a moving target in the extremities is almost impossible. Every trained officer knows, even if you could make that shot, there would be fallout from that round continuing to travel or worse striking an innocent bystander. For that type of shooting you will have to go to the movies or watch T.V.

There are quite a few misconceptions surrounding police officers. Most are derived from media entertainment, some from rumors, others from hate.

Police officers are trained to chase a subject that suddenly takes off running, not to start shooting. Police officers in an urban environment save more lives than they take. The average police officer will not shoot anyone in his or her entire career. Try that on for size.

In a police officer's full career, he or she will write enough reports and fill out enough forms to fill an entire library.

Another shocking fact is there are some police officers that do not like to write tickets. In an urban city like Detroit, most officers do not have the time to write tickets. They are too busy making emergency calls. Still, to this very day, Detroit's 911 emergency operators answer more calls than New York!

Did you know that a police officer's life is in danger from the moment they leave the police station? When we sit down to eat, when we stop to write a report, whenever we pull up to an address on a run, when we enter an apartment building, while doing traffic, while stopping a vehicle on the freeway or the surface streets, before you can even talk to a driver. You can be run down simply by accident, while on foot patrol, entering a bank, or a local liquor store, while routinely cruising the city streets day or night. In or out of your scout car, we are in danger of being ambushed.

These are just a few of the ways we won't make it home at shifts end. When we are back at the precinct station we can finally make a sigh of relief. How would you like this to be your day at the office?

Taking all of this into consideration remember: you never know when you will be faced with that life and death situation; when in less than a split second you will have to kill or be killed. You may have to kill to save your partner or an innocent citizen. You might even have to kill to protect a prisoner. It has happened and whatever decision you make will impact or change your life forever. Therefore, we must realize this license to kill is not a Gift. Instead, it is a great responsibility to be used as skillfully as a surgeon to cut out the cancer of crime.

A supervisor once told me that I should buy a holster with a large flap to cover up my 44, because it scared the citizens. I told him that the only ones that were scared were the criminals who needed to be shot.

I do find that one of the most misunderstood circumstances arise from unintended mistakes caused by extreme emotions on both sides. There are good citizens who have never been in trouble with the police who get physical when no weapons were involved with officers but resulted in serious altercations. By the same token, there are police officers who have never committed unnecessarily aggressive physical violence on any citizen that would appear to have committed police brutality. However, as I have mentioned before, when an officer makes a mistake or goes too far, all officers are blamed.

Even now, as I have previously mentioned, this same type of blame is placed on minorities. When and how can this wrong be righted? As an officer, you sometimes feel you are damned if you do react or dead if you don't!!

Chapter 41

ATTORNEYS AFTER THE LAW

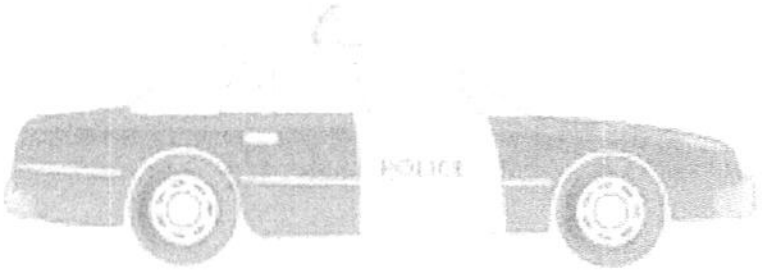

It was a warm sunny day in the middle of May. "13-4, make this location at this bar; meet a complainant for an R.A. report (robbery armed)!" Readers, are you ready? Let's go!

As we pull up to the location, several people are milling around outside a bar on Woodward Ave.

When we enter the location given by dispatch, we can hear the complainant crying about two hold up men who took his income tax money.

We observed that the victim has cuts and bruises about his head, evident from the attack associated with the vicious hold up.

My partner and I interviewed the complainant who stated that if we caught the perps he would not be afraid to be our prosecuting witness.

We exited the bar and sat in the cruiser writing a report, when one the ladies of the evening gestured for us to meet her around the corner a block away. She stated she was aware of our police work in the area and appreciated our efforts to be fair and impartial and to show it.

When we met her around the corner, she gave us info on the two hold up men, their names, and where to find them.

Now, it's time for you, our third-party riders, to remain in the car while my partner and I attempt to make a most dangerous felony arrest.

We notified dispatch of our location and intentions to investigate, and that we were going in without back up while we had the element of surprise.

We simply knocked on the door, asking for one of the names we were given.

As soon as we heard the lock turn, we made an all-out surprise attack overpowering both criminals.

With an eye witness and a complainant, and a well written report, we now knew we had an airtight case.

Later, we found out that there was one other component to this case. Before the hold up, the complainant was bragging in the bar about his income tax check and how much money he had in front of all of the patrons, including the holdup men.

In about a month, we were summoned to court. My partner and I were very upbeat.

Once in the court room, the prosecutor called us over to his table. He was looking uncomfortable. He told us we would not be needed. Now, we were uncomfortable. He told us we no longer had a complainant.

We said, "That's not possible. He's right here in the room with us."

The prosecutor said, "Sit down and watch."

They called our case. The two perps were there as well.

The judge asked our so-called complainant about the day in question. He said he remembered the day, but couldn't recall who robbed him.

The prosecutor pointed out the two punks sitting with their lawyer and put the question to him again.

The liar looked down and said he had never seen the two before.

The judge was furious. He said this was a travesty of justice and he knew what was taking place. Then he thanked my partner and me for good and proper police work and told us we were dismissed. He warned the lowlifes if they were ever brought before his jurisdiction again there would be hell to pay.

The prosecutor caught us in the hall and broke down what had taken place. It just so happened that the defending attorney had actually paid our complainant his money back in return for his loss of memory! There is a two-pronged reason for this kind of deceit. The defense attorney wins his case and the criminals, in addition to his fee, must repay the attorney for the amount of the theft. Now, the two hold up men, not being gainfully employed, you guess where they will get the money.

The next incident occurred while I was assigned to C.O.S. at 1300 Beaubien in downtown Detroit.

CHAPTER FORTY-ONE - "Attorney after the Law"

There is a pay parking lot across the street from headquarters that was not used on platoon one. I had parked there on this particular night. As I was dispatching, one of my coworkers ran up to tell me someone was breaking into my vehicle. Our locker room windows were directly across from this lot.

I called for a scout car to make the location, while I headed for the elevator to back up the scout car.

By the time I had made it to the scene, they had the perp in the back seat of the scout car and told him, "You see that large officer coming this way? That is his vehicle you broke into?"

The perp started screaming for help.

Unfortunately, I couldn't work him over because a sergeant had just pulled up.

As usual, about a month later, I was called to court about my case. I was off duty that morning so I was wearing plain clothes.

I walked into the hall and sat down waiting to be called, when I saw the criminal walk up and sit almost across from me. Not knowing who I was, he began a conversation with one of the attorneys also waiting to be called.

Watching his demeanor and listening to the perp's conversation, I surmised that the perp knew his way around the court system. He began to tell this lawyer, who was not his attorney, how he had a bad day and broke into a police officer's van.

I was already familiar with what it was like to be a victim of crime in this city, however, to sit and listen to a career criminal make light of victimizing a police officer made me aware of my hard earned discipline to control my power and authority.

Once in court, my case was finally called up. But instead of calling me to the stand, it was brought to the attention of the court that my case was put on hold. The perp had committed two more vehicle-related crimes after my case that were given more priority.

So there you have it. Remember, career criminals are quite familiar with the system, almost as much as their attorneys!

42 Chapter

THE NO SNITCH RULE

Again, as I continue to write, more deaths and killings interrupt my literary progress. Two criminals in a stolen vehicle brandishing a gun were observed by the police. Knowing the officers spotted the weapon, the perps took off at a high rate of speed. You are in the scout with us as this event takes place. However, let's put this on hold for a few.

What is it that the fine citizens of Detroit want of their police officers? To stop violent criminals in their footsteps, take guns and other deadly weapons away from these killers, to protect the citizenry at all cost, to come to any dangerous situation whenever we are called, to put our lives on the line without hesitation, to fight with, shoot it out with, and to arrest the most dangerous criminals in the United States, and to pursue them to the ends of North America, Canada, and the Mexican border, if necessary.

Therefore, when we see a felony taking place right before our eyes, what should we do? What do you as citizens expect us to do? What does a criminal expect us to do? When a criminal commits a felony, or any other violent crime, does he or she know right from wrong?

Knowing that the perps are dead wrong and in the commission of a crime, they purposely injure or kill innocents in the process of their crime or attempted escape, why is it that most of the citizens blame the police? How is it that these lowlifes who set out to destroy you and your families and loved ones; who show and have no remorse for what they do to you, your life, limb or property, become the neighborhood heroes for some and the police become the enemy?

This phenomenon is taking place all over Detroit at neighborhood block parties where these cowards shoot into crowds of men, women and children with no regard for who is killed or injured.

As I write this, there have been three such shootings in Detroit in one week. Here is the worst part: no one will cooperate with the police. And while they are not hurting the police, they are helping the criminals to do further violence. Yes, there are those who actually believe that they are helping their community by siding with the law breakers that are victimizing their very community.

One thing is certain, the police of your community will not threaten to kill you for not exposing the ones who kill the very innocents that will make a positive difference in your lives. Just try to justify the logic. Imagine the total pain of your child dying before you. This is not the norm as you well know. So explain to me, how would you as a trained police officer, respond to total violence when you are confronted for no other reason than you are wearing a police uniform? Yes, it is as simple as wearing even a private guard uniform that appears to make you out to be a police officer, because the typical criminal only sees what he or she thinks is someone there to stop their criminal activities or take them back to prison.

What I have described is so very dangerous to any and all law enforcement officers, and it is so life-threatening that you must do whatever is possible to protect yourselves.

Keep in mind that quite a few of our law-abiding citizens simply hate police because of traffic or parking tickets alone, or have been raised in a household that taught them to hate. Sounds closely familiar to racism, doesn't it?

A war between the community and police officers is one we can ill afford, simply because it is the criminals who would benefit. Think about it! However, when and if the community joins forces with the police, there is nowhere the criminals who prey on you and I can hide. We are more powerful than these cowardly criminals, but they pick on us one by one. Here again, that is why we must stand together, neighbor-by-neighbor, block-by-block, community-by-community, city-by-city. They cannot exist where we shed a bright light on their criminal activities. If you have no support system, unite yourself with some neighbor that does. Set up a communications network by phone or computer. This is a powerful tool and easy to do. Most of all, it is a secret weapon that even retirees and the elderly can do. Don't underestimate our senior citizens. Remember, growing old is not for wimps and it does not take a body builder to pull a trigger, or learn to be a proficient shot!

As you may suspect, this writer is not going to go over well with the criminal element, but what the hell, I never did. Nevertheless, it was their aggression that led to their demise, not ours, and certainly not yours, my good citizens.

As a police officer grows older, retired or active, he or she becomes even more dangerous, just as an old gunfighter or peace officer. Why? Because they have survived so many battles over their careers and can read a dangerous situation like you and I can read a book.

This information and the violent events I have shared with you will not grow old. As I have previously mentioned, there have been three block party shootings in one week, a young man recently shot in the head and then robbed of his sunglasses and flip flops. Why? What the hell does a cowardly punk think that the taking of an innocent life can profit him? What benefit can he possibly obtain from the cold-blooded killing he set out to do and commit one of man's greatest crimes against man in return for these material objects?

This type of illogical reality escapes me, as a law enforcement officer and a born and raised citizen of Detroit. I detest this type of wasteful violence which angers me to my core. Just like any concerned officer, I sometimes wish I could be everywhere at once so that I could stop all crime in its tracks.

Again, as I write, the news is actively reporting that the police are looking for a rapist that broke in the window of a child's window and took her out of the house and raped this innocent.

Please forgive me for being so passionate about this so called "no snitch rule." It is not snitching when you report the witnessing of a crime. As you can see, so many crimes are occurring that they are interrupting my train of thought.

Now back to the crooks with the gun. You are with us as they take off at a high rate of speed. However, as they enter a residential neighborhood, we back off calling out the description and location.

Not bothering to look back, the two crooks race through the quiet community, eventually plowing through innocent people with fatal results. As the police arrive, both crooks are eventually captured. This is an ongoing murder case, so I will stop here. By the way, the weapon was also recovered.

Have no fear. We will not stop in the pursuit of these lawless hoodlums. We do not know how to quit when our right to live a safe life is concerned.

Chapter 43

THE BIG FOUR

Out of the many specialized police units, which include the civic center units, stationary traffic units, central tow (better known as C-tow, a police operated tow truck) operating in the downtown area, 30 series booster cars, 40 series one man cars, motor traffic freeway and accident cars, motorcycles, (for traffic control, funeral and motorcade escorts), X-cars, (specializing in all types of traffic accidents; one in every precinct) fatal squad, (deadly accident specialists), 80 series gun cars, (loaded with long guns and ammo, for back up in a fire fight), PSU (precinct support unit, better known as STRESS), mounted division, officers on horses trained in crowd control), Women's Division, (based in headquarters, investigating rapes, child abuse, fully trained and armed with all police powers) bomb squad, MOG heavy tow, precinct detectives division, plain clothes and cars, working out of all precinct stations, and last but not least the infamous BIG FOUR (a full-size black, four door cruiser with no emergency lights, most crews members were over six foot, three plain clothes officers and one uniform officer, the driver stays with the car at all times, in the trunk a 45 cal. machine gun). This unit was formed to hunt the worst of the criminals in the early 1950's. However, it wasn't long before they gained a reputation of ill repute in the neighborhoods. The officers were not well liked. Even worse, they were feared by the law-abiding citizens. I personally had two run-ins with The Big Four, as an adolescent and later a teen driver.

There was one cruiser in every precinct. By the 1970's, the cruisers were beginning to fade out; but before that happened, your writer was chosen as a crew member on the cruiser. Yes, it's true. I was the uniform driver of my precinct's cruiser. In my excitement, I came in on my own time and perked up the engine in the police garage. My senior crew noticed the difference right away and was pleased. We did not incur the wrath of the community, as in the days of old. Sadly, it wasn't long before our cruiser was shut down as well.

44 Chapter

THE BLUE PIGS

I did not check the origin of the police band known as The Blue Pigs; however, with my 1970 beginning on the force, they were prolific. They had already made a name for themselves, singing and playing music in full uniform. To visualize Detroit Police Officers as entertainers fascinated me as much as it did their child audiences.

Working in conjunction with P.A.L (Police Athletic League), they seemed to be everywhere. As far as the citizens were concerned, they had reached rock band status. Everyone that watched their shows were ecstatic. I was asked about them quite often as I patrolled the streets. They were no passing fancy. They were truly loved and surprisingly talented. What made them almost magical was that the officers liked what they were doing. Even as I write, I would love to see another show. I am a life-long fan.

The band faded out for a while, however, there is encouraging news that they will make a comeback. Their talent and enthusiasm definitely helped police-community relations then and now. Their return would be just what the doctor ordered.

45 Epilogue

This writing is some 45 years in the making, and yet most of these past incidences are as timely and up to date as today's news. The violent crimes have not changed, just the faces, genders and ages of our child and infant victims. There is one overriding factor: the DPD has not had these depleted numbers in over 100 years. Believe me, attention to this reality will spark change!

There were almost 70 student patrolmen and one student policewoman in my academy class. At the end of twenty-five years, there were only four of us present to receive a gold retirement ring from the union. The union president made a big deal of what it takes to achieve this milestone. My career continued another ten years with the force.

My hope in revealing for the first time in Detroit a police officer's inner feelings and some of the different encounters that I faced, has given you my ride along reader a living realistic heart beating, out of your body into my world, that clutches at every breath you take as we became one in the streets of the "D!"

Officers, remember, there are so many ways to get into a dangerous situation that it would be difficult to count them. New dangers and violence continue to arise. Keep in mind the threat is real, ever present, and in this arena we are the outnumbered gladiators. Bring your five senses to bear on all contacts, and when you have survived long enough you will begin to develop that sixth sense to deal with that eerie existence of awaiting danger.

Although I was powerless to ease all of the pain and suffering, I was able to transfer a lot of it to the perpetrators. Every day is a fight for survival for some officer somewhere in the U.S. When you brave those unpredictable streets headed for the unknown, remember: you are not alone. I ride with you 24-7, 365!

To this end, we must face any danger put before us and vindicate that responsibility in the line of duty. From the inspiration of magnificent courage and the sacrifice for that ideal has emerged "AN AMERICAN CRIMEFIGHTER" representing "BLUE KNIGHTS IN THE D." In a city that never sleeps, the action in this true life account has just begun. So have the efforts of our HEROES IN BLUE! While I have made it my life's work to protect others, I have learned that only GOD can protect me. His impenetrable shield has spared my life many times over! I lack the words to properly praise Him. He knows my spirit, soul and body are His!

I have written this work as a legacy for all of my loved ones, co-worker, readers and their generations and to leave a chronicle of my love for all mankind. It is my fervent wish that all of my positive readers will find a warm place in their hearts for the officers of the DPD who are loved and sometimes hated so much. We are the thin line between you and total unbridled violence. At times, just as any other humans, we can be so angry that we become infuriated with a murderous rage toward some of the criminals we encounter. And yet on the other end of the scale is the heart-wrenching pity we feel for the poor, the homeless, the lonely and elderly with no one to turn to and, worst of all, hungry, neglected and children. These conditions rip at our humanity, exposing our true hidden inner strength and compassion. These thoughts pass through every urban crime stopper's mind at one time or another. However, the control not to exterminate those who might deserve it, and yet to feel pain for those who suffer from crime and or poverty; in a color blind uniform, is the true essence of a returning hero. An American Crime fighter from the "D"!

I hope this ride along hasn't freaked you out. I hope that putting you right in the action, but not the danger, has opened your eyes to some of the encounters of street justice. Somehow I feel that you have a greater understanding of my attitude toward enforcing the law.

I have not touched on all of the evil aspects we have witnessed. I feel that would be a bit to inhumane, or let us give it an (R) rating, even for you adults. However, even as we are killed for something we did not do, we take pride in protecting you to the best of our ability and will continue to put ourselves in harm's way to defend your families.

Although we are not rushing to meet death, we know the strong possibility exists. That is why training from our senior officers is so crucial. The next time you see one of us on our beat remember we are human also. We are sons and daughters, husbands and wives, fathers and mothers, uncles and aunts, grandfathers and grandmothers, friends and even some of your neighbors.

One of my goals is to bring reason, compromise, and humility out of hate and violence. Nothing is possible without God, my Shield and Lightening Power against evil. Regardless of the politics of the day, ours is an American cause. We must defend the defenseless.

Finally, consider this: when a police officer is cold-bloodedly and brutally ambushed and murdered, why are there no riots, no protests or demonstrations except for family, friends and co-workers. Who cares enough to dignify the outrage?

In the latter months of 2016, there were three police officers murdered in Detroit. In the first six months of 2017, six more officers have been shot. We are now nearing the end of June and one officer is still fighting for his life. This means Detroit leads the nation in officer ambush shootings.

NATIONAL LAW ENFORCEMENT OFFICERS MEMORIAL FUND
RESPECT.HONOR.REMEMBER
HONORING 394 AMERICAN LAW ENFORCEMENT HEROES

On May 13, 2017, the 29th Annual Candlelight Vigil at the National Law Enforcement Officers Memorial in Washington, D.C. honored 394 who have died in the line of duty. The names were read out loud; 143 of those officers died last year. The other 251 died before 2016, but their names had never been added to the memorial.

U.S. Attorney General Jeff Sessions and Department of Homeland Security Secretary John Kelly spoke at the event and lead the crowd in the candle lighting.

With this year's additions, there are now 21,183 names engraved on the memorial. The names represent all 50 states as well as the District of Columbia, U.S. territories, federal law enforcement and military police agencies.

For more information, go to any one of the sources listed below.

Source: 394 Fallen Officers Honored During DC's Police Week Vigil | NBC4 Washington http://www.nbcwashington.com/news/national-international/Thousands-Expected-in-Washington-DC-Saturday-for-Fallen-Officer-Memorial-422181863.html#ixzz4h5tKtVtV

Follow us: @nbcwashington on Twitter | NBCWashington on Facebook

46

Honoring American Law Enforcement Heros

Allow me to add that in the first five months here in Michigan four officers have been killed and one is still clinging to life at the time of this writing.

ALABAMA

KENNETH LEVELLA BETTIS
Alabama Department of Corrections
CHARLES LEE SIMS
Butler County, Alabama, S.O.
TROY CLIFTON WILLINGHAM
Cleburne County, Alabama, S.O.
GEORGE ARNOLD SCOTT
DeKalb County, Alabama, S.O.
ELBERT R ABERNATHY
Jefferson County, Alabama. S.O.
JOHN WESLEY O'BRYEN
Etowah County, Alabama, S.O.
EDWIN ANTHONY KIRBY
Jackson County, Alabama, S.O.
CHARLES HAGGERTY
Mobile, Alabama, P.D.
LUTHER THOMAS BOZEMAN
Shelby County, Alabama, S.O.
JOHN WILLIAM BURK
Talladega County, Alabama, S.O.
HOLLIS BROWN HORTON
Tuscaloosa County, Alabama, S.O.

ALASKA
ALLEN DAVID BRANDT
Fairbanks, Alaska, P.D.
ARIZONA
JOHN MCCARTY
Arizona Game & Fish Department
LEANDER FRANK
Navajo Nation, P.D.
DAVID VAN GLASSER
Phoenix, Arizona, P.D.
DARRIN LEE REED
Show Low, Arizona, P.D.
ARKANSAS
ROBERT AARON BARKER
McCrory, Arkansas, P.D.
LISA ANNE MAULDIN
Miller County, Arkansas, S.O.
JAMES MATT LAWRENCE
Osceola, Arkansas, P.D.
BARNEY STIEL
Pulaski County, Arkansas, S.O.
GILBERT BYRD BURCHFIELD
Saline County, Arkansas, S.O.
WILLIAM PRESSLEY COOPER
Sebastian County, Arkansas, S.O.
CALIFORNIA
NATHAN DANIEL TAYLOR
California Highway Patrol
ROD BARRON LUCAS
Fresno County, California, S.O
CHARLES W WINSTON
Los Angeles County, California, C.O.
FREDERICK F MOORE
Los Angeles County, California, M.O.
ALFONSO LOPEZ
Los Angeles County, California, S.O.

ARTHUR J SOLOMON
Los Angeles County, California, S.O.
STEVEN C OWEN
Los Angeles County, California, S.O.
JACK LANCESON HOPKINS
Modoc County, California, S.O.
PAUL MICHAEL CARLISLE
Oakland, California, P.D.
JOSE GILBERTO VEGA
Palm Springs, California, P.D.
LESLEY MARIE ZEREBNY
Palm Springs, California, P.D.
FRANK A LUNGERSHAUSEN
Sacramento, California, P.D.
JONATHAN MATIAS DE GUZMAN
San Diego, California, P.D.
MICHAEL JASON KATHERMAN
San Jose, California, P.D.
DENNIS RANDALL WALLACE
Stanislaus County, California, S.D.
SCOTT ALFRED BALLANTYNE
Tulare County, California, S.O.
COLORADO
CODY JAMES DONAHUE
Colorado State Patrol
DEREK MACE GEER
Mesa County, Colorado, S.O.
NATHANIEL ALAN CARRIGAN
Park County, Colorado, S.O.
CONNECTICUT
RALPH COSMER YOUNG
Connecticut Dept. of Motor Vehicle
CORNELIUS RAIN
Alachua County, Florida, S.O.
WILLIAM ARTHUR MAY
Alachua County, Florida, S.O.

JOHN HENRY WIGGINS
DeSoto County, Florida, S.O.
JORGE RAMOS
Florida Department of Corrections
MOSES A HILL
Gulf County, Florida, S.O.
JOHN ROBERT KOTFILA JR
Hillsborough County, Florida, S.O.
JORGE SANCHEZ
Miami, Florida, P.D.
HENRY MALCOLM MCALEENAN JR
Miami-Dade, Florida, P.D.
MYRLE A WHIDDEN
Mulberry, Florida, C.O.
ERIC JAMES OLIVER
Nassau County, Florida, S.O.
SEBASTIAN EDWARD DIANA
Orange County, Florida, S.O.
MICHAEL SCOTT WILLIAMS
Taylor County, Florida, S.O.

GEORGIA

NICHOLAS RYAN SMARR
Americus, Georgia,P.D.
WILLIAM CYRUS BARROW
Americus, Georgia, P.D.
WILLIAM R MORRIS
Americus, Georgia, P.D.
ANTHONY JOSEPH FREEMAN
Bibb County, Georgia, S.O.
JUSTIN LEVI ROUSE
Boston, Georgia, P.D.
TIMOTHY KEVIN SMITH
Eastman, Georgia, P.D.
DA'JHAUN GAITORS
Georgia Department of Corrections
JODY CARL SMITH

Georgia Southwestern State University P.D.
LORIE JAMES MANGHAM SR
Lamar County, Georgia, S.O.
JUSTIN SCOTT WHITE
Newton County, Georgia, S.O.
DARYL WAYNE SMALLWOOD
Peach County, Georgia, S.O.
PATRICK MICHAEL SONDRON
Peach County, Georgia, S.O.
GREGORY EUGENE BARNEY
Riverdale, Georgia, P.D.
JOHN C PARRISH
Walker County, Georgia, S.O.

IDAHO
EUGENE TAYLOR
Bannock County, Idaho, S.O.
W J MCFADDEN
Bannock County, Idaho, S.O.
ELBERT P SWEET
Bingham County, Idaho, S.O.
WALTER COFFIN
Boise County, Idaho, S.O.
SCOTT W PALMER
Clearwater County, Idaho, S.O.
MORLEY H CANNON
Fruitland, Idaho, P.D.
NATHAN HERBERT SUITTER
Gem County, Idaho, S.O.
CHARLES H TORRANCE
Power County, Idaho. S.O.
ILLINOIS
JAMES IRWIN BROCKMEYER
Chester, Illinois, P.D.
AUSTIN L FITCH
Chicago, Illinois, P.D.

PATRICK JOSEPH MCGANN JR
Chicago, Illinois, P.D.
WILLIAM FEELEY
Chicago, Illinois, P.D.
GEORGE JOSEPH TURLEY
Cook County Jail, Illinois
JASON GALLERO
Cook County Sheriff's, Illinois, P.D.
WALTER PATRICK MCCARTHY
Cook County Sheriff's, Illinois, P.D.
HENRY C WESTLUND
Cook County, Illinois, Highway Police
ROBERT MANN STAFFORD
Cook County, Illinois, Highway Police
ROBERT VINCENT WHISENAND
Dixon, Illinois, P.D.
J WILLIAM BARNES
Macoupin County, Illinois, S.O.
ADAM SCOTT CONRAD
Marion County, Illinois S.O.
SCOT FITZGERALD
South Jacksonville, Illinois, P.D.

INDIANA

CARL ALLEN KOONTZ
Howard County, Indiana, S.O.
WILLIAM ROLLIN BRAND
Monroe County, Indiana, S.O.

IOWA

ANTHONY DAVID BEMINIO
Des Moines, Iowa, P.D.
CARLOS BERNABE PUENTE-MORALES
Des Moines, Iowa, P.D.
DAVID ALLEN BOWEN
Des Moines, Iowa, P.D.
SUSAN LOUISE FARRELL
Des Moines, Iowa, P.D.
THOMAS NICHOLSON
Gowrie, Iowa, P.D.

ROBERT FERN MCKINLEY
Pottawattamie County, Iowa, S.O.
WARREN T HODGINS
Sioux City, Iowa, P.D.
JUSTIN SCOTT MARTIN
Urbandale, Iowa, P.D.
ADAM DEAN LIDDLE
Waterloo, Iowa, P.D.
SHAWN GLENN MILLER
West Des Moines, Iowa, P.D.

KANSAS

CHARLES SCHRAM
El Dorado, Kansas, P.D.
BRANDON SCOTT COLLINS
Johnson County, Kansas, S.O.
BRAD D LANCASTER
Kansas City, Kansas, P.D.
ROBERT DAVID MELTON
Kansas City, Kansas, P.D.
JAMES MICHAEL BUFFUM
Topeka, Kansas, P.D.

KENTUCKY

JOHN GILLIAM
Cumberland, Kentucky, P.D.
DOLIE CLIFFORD HARMON
Johnson County, Kentucky, S.O.
CHARLES DAVID HOWLEY
Oldham County, Kentucky, P.D.
JAMES CLEM
Poor Fork, Kentucky, P.D.
PRESTON C RAINS
Whitley County, Kentucky, C.O.

LOUISIANA

MATTHEW LANE GERALD
Baton Rouge, Louisiana, P.D.
MONTRELL JACKSON

Baton Rouge, Louisiana, P.D.
BRADFORD ALLEN GARAFOLA SR
East Baton Rouge Parish, Louisiana, S.O.
SHANNON MATTHEW BROWN
Fenton, Louisiana, P.D.
DAVID F MICHEL JR
Jefferson Parish, Louisiana, S.O.
JUDE WILLIAMS LEWIS
New Orleans, Louisiana, P.D.
NATASHA MARIA HUNTER
New Orleans, Louisiana, P.D.
THOMAS J ALBERT SR
New Orleans, Louisiana, P.D.
DAVID KYLE ELAHI
Sterlington, Louisiana, P.D.
DERRICK MORIAL MINGO
Winnsboro, Louisiana, P.D.

MAINE

RENE ALBERT GOUPIL
Maine State Police

MARYLAND

CHARLES W FISHER
Baltimore City, Maryland, P.D.
HERBERT BITZEL
Baltimore City, Maryland, P.D.
JOHN O'MAYER
Baltimore City, Maryland, P.D.
JOSEPH C WALDSACHS
Baltimore City, Maryland, P.D.
MICHAEL J EGAN
Baltimore City, Maryland, P.D.
MICHAEL J BURNS
Baltimore City, Maryland, P.D.
THOMAS H WORTHINGTON
Baltimore City, Maryland, P.D.
MARK FRANKLIN LOGSDON

Harford County, Maryland, S.O.
PATRICK BRYAN DAILEY
Harford County, Maryland, S.O.
EDWARD CLARENCE WILSON
North Beach, Maryland, P.D.
JACAI DAVID COLSON
Prince George's County, Maryland, P.D.
MASSACHUSETTS
LOUIS DUNCAN PHIPPS
Ashland, Massachusetts, P.D.
RONALD TARENTINO JR
Auburn, Massachusetts, P.D.
EDWARD THOMAS RICHARD LANDERS
Barnstable, Massachusetts, P.D.
CHARLES EDWARD BRADLEY
Cambridge, Massachusetts, P.D.
JOSEPH ANTHONY RIBEIRO SR
Massachusetts Department of Correction
THOMAS L CLARDY
Massachusetts State Police
WILLIAM H FURDON
Newton, Massachusetts, P.D.
BENJAMIN JOHN VOSS
Somerset, Massachusetts, P.D.
RICHARD TERENCE DEVER
Suffolk County, Massachusetts, S.O.
MICHIGAN
JOSEPH PETER ZANGARO
Berrien County, Michigan, Trial Court
RONALD E KIENZLE
Berrien County, Michigan, Trial Court
MICHAEL ARTHUR WINTER
Branch County, Michigan, S.O.
KENNETH MELVIN STEIL
Detroit, Michigan, P.D.

KEVIN DWAYNE MILLER
Detroit, Michigan, P.D.
MYRON ANTHONY JARRETT
Detroit, Michigan, P.D.
JOSEPH J MURRAY
Huron County, Michigan, S.O.
COLLIN JAMES ROSE
Wayne State University P.D.

MINNESOTA

LOWELL LLOYD KRAUSE
Amboy, Minnesota, P.D.
DOUGLAS EUGENE CLAASSEN
Hayfield, Minnesota, P.D.
CHARLES C CHANNELS
Minneapolis, Minnesota, P.D.
JAMES L GARDNER
Osseo, Minnesota, P.D.

MISSISSIPPI

JOHN RUSSELL HARRIS
Hinds County, Mississippi, S.O.
JAMES LEE TARTT
Mississippi Bureau of Narcotics
B M MILLSTEAD
Richton, Mississippi, P.D.
WILLIAM LAWRENCE DUNNAM
Richton, Mississippi, P.D.
CLARENCE JAMES LANIER
Warren County, Mississippi, S.O.

MISSOURI

ANDREW JACKSON RUSSELL
Campbell Twp, Missouri, C.O.
CHARLES J KINSER
Greene County, Missouri, S.O.
JOHN HENRY KELLER
Greene County, Missouri, S.O.

RONALD EUGENE STRITTMATTER
Lakeshire, Missouri, P.D.
S DAVID NELSON
Pleasant Hill, Missouri, P.D.
PAUL ALLEN CLARK
St. Francois County, Missouri, S.O.
BLAKE CURTIS SNYDER
St. Louis County, Missouri, P.D.

NEBRASKA

GREGORY KEITH HAMILL
Omaha, Nebraska, P.D.

NEW HAMPSHIRE

JOHN STRATTON WALKER SR
Cheshire County, New Hampshire, S.O.

MINNESOTA

LOWELL LLOYD KRAUSE
Amboy, Minnesota, P.D.
DOUGLAS EUGENE CLAASSEN
Hayfield, Minnesota, P.D.
CHARLES C CHANNELS
Minneapolis, Minnesota, P.D.
JAMES L GARDNER
Osseo, Minnesota, P.D.

MISSISSIPPI

JOHN RUSSELL HARRIS
Hinds County, Mississippi, S.O.
JAMES LEE TARTT
Mississippi Bureau of Narcotics
B M MILLSTEAD
Richton, Mississippi, P.D.
WILLIAM LAWRENCE DUNNAM
Richton, Mississippi, P.D.
CLARENCE JAMES LANIER
Warren County, Mississippi, S.O.

MISSOURI

ANDREW JACKSON RUSSELL

Campbell Twp, Missouri, C.O.
CHARLES J KINSER
Greene County, Missouri, S.O.
JOHN HENRY KELLER
Greene County, Missouri, S.O.
RONALD EUGENE STRITTMATTER
Lakeshire, Missouri, P.D.
S DAVID NELSON
Pleasant Hill, Missouri, P.D.
PAUL ALLEN CLARK
St. Francois County, Missouri, S.O.
BLAKE CURTIS SNYDER
St. Louis County, Missouri, P.D.
NEBRASKA
GREGORY KEITH HAMILL
Omaha, Nebraska, P.D.
NEW HAMPSHIRE
JOHN STRATTON WALKER SR
Cheshire County, New Hampshire, S.O.
NEW JERSEY
NIKEELAN SEMMON
New Jersey Department of Corrections
FRANKIE LAMAR WILLIAMS
New Jersey State Police
SEAN EAMONN CULLEN
New Jersey State Police
WILLIAM GEORGE FEARON
New Jersey State Police
JOHN MARK CORTAZZO
Port Authority of New York/New Jersey, P.D.
NEW MEXICO
CLINT E CORVINUS
Alamogordo, New Mexico, P.D.
JOSE ISMAEL CHAVEZ
Hatch, New Mexico, P.D.
APOLONIO PINO

Santa Fe, New Mexico, P.D.
JOSE ANTONIO GRIEGO
RYAN SEAN THOMAS
Valencia County, New Mexico, S.O.
NEW YORK
BARTHOLOMEW PURDY
New York City Dept. of Correction
HUGH MCGOVERN
New York City Dept. of Correction
JEREMIAH MURPHY
New York City Dept. of Correction
PETER A MALLON
New York City Dept. of Correction
WILLIAM MCCONNELL
New York City Dept. of Correction
ALEX W BAEZ
New York City, New York, P.D.
ALICK W HERRMANN
New York City, New York, P.D.
ANGEL ANTONIO CREAGH
New York City, New York, P.D.
ROBERT A ZANE JR
New York City, New York, P.D.
ROBERT B HELMKE
New York City, New York, P.D.
ROBERT M EHMER
New York City, New York, P.D.
ROBERT V OSWAIN JR
New York City, New York, P.D.
ROBERT W WILLIAMSON
New York City, New York, P.D.
ROBERTO L RIVERA
New York City, New York, P.D.
RONALD G BECKER JR
New York City, New York, P.D.
SANDRA Y ADRIAN

New York City, New York, P.D.
STEPHEN P SCALZA
New York City, New York, P.D.
STEVEN HOM
New York City, New York, P.D.
STUART F FISHKIN
New York City, New York, P.D.
VITO S MAURO
New York City, New York, P.D.
WILLIAM J HOLFESTER
New York City, New York, P.D.
NANCY VIAL
New York State Dept. of Corrections
NELLIE WICKS
New York State Dept. of Corrections
SAMUEL CALVERT
New York State Dept. of Corrections
COVEL CHASE PIERCE
New York State Police
PAUL R STUEWER
New York State Police
TIMOTHY P PRATT
New York State Police
FRED GHUSSIN
NY County, New York, District Attorney's Office
WILLIAM F CULLEN
NYC Board of Water Supply, P.D.
KERRY JOSEPH WINTERS SR
Ulster County, New York, S.O.
ANTHONY MAGGIORE
Yonkers, New York, P.D.

NORTH CAROLINA

JOHN THOMAS ISENHOUR
Forsyth County, North Carolina, S.O.
AMOS MONROE BORDEAUX
North Carolina Wildlife Resources Commission

GROVER CLEVELAND QUINN JR
North Carolina Wildlife Resources Commission
JOSEPH D WHITAKER
North Carolina Wildlife Resources Commission
WILLIAM G HOLLER
North Carolina Wildlife Resources Commission
CHARLIE WELLS DUNN
Scotland Neck, North Carolina, P.D.
TIMOTHY JAMES BRACKEEN
Shelby, North Carolina, P.D.

NORTH DAKOTA

JASON DAVID MOSZER
Fargo, North Dakota, P.D.

OHIO

FRANK WILSON
Beverly, Ohio, P.D.
JOHN M CONE
Canfield, Ohio, P.D.
AARON JACKSON CHRISTIAN
Chesapeake, Ohio, P.D.
FREDERICK FRANK KUNDTS
Columbus, Ohio, Division of Police
JOHN MANNING
Columbus, Ohio, Division of Police
STEVEN MICHAEL SMITH
Columbus, Ohio, Division of Police
THOMAS WAYNE COTTRELL JR
Danville, Ohio, P.D.
CARL MAYES ETHERINGTON
Granville, Ohio, P.D.
SEAN RICHARD JOHNSON
Hilliard Division of Police, Ohio
ROY E CARTER
Miami Twp, Ohio, P.D.
KENNETH VELEZ
Ohio State Highway Patrol

OKLAHOMA
ROBERT PATRICK FLICKINGER
Chickasaw Lighthorse, Oklahoma, P.D.
WILLIAM DUTTON HUTCHINS
Claremore, Oklahoma, P.D.
JOHN LOUIS WILSON
Nowata, Oklahoma, P.D.
TREY BRENON PRITCHARD
Sapulpa, Oklahoma, P.D.
OREGON
JASON MICHAEL GOODDING
Seaside, Oregon P.D.
PENNSYLVANIA
ANDREW J CONROY
Allegheny County, Pennsylvania, C.O.
JOHN MANCOS
Allegheny County, Pennsylvania, C.O.
MARTIN F WINDT
Allegheny County, Pennsylvania, C.O.
THOMAS J O'SULLIVAN
Allegheny County, Pennsylvania, C.O.
FRANK X MOONEY
Allegheny County, Pennsylvania, S.O.
MEYER VAN LEWEN
SCOTT LESLIE BASHIOUM
Canonsburg Borough, Pennsylvania, P.D.
EDWARD A WEHE III
Delaware County Park Police, Pennsylvania
JAMES GOLDEN
Dunmore, Pennsylvania, P.D.
LLOYD ELWOOD YODER
Everett, Pennsylvania, P.D.
ANTHONY MASLOWSKI
Exeter Borough, Pennsylvania, P.D.
GEORGE DWORSKI
Exeter Borough, Pennsylvania, P.D.

ALVIN BARRETT
Houtzdale, Pennsylvania, P.D.
SAMUEL B ELDRIDGE
Johnstown, Pennsylvania, P.D.
PETER GRIFFIN
Lock Haven, Pennsylvania, P.D.
KRISTOPHER DAVID MOULES
Luzerne County Correctional Facility, Pennsylvania
MILAN BARBER
Minersville, Pennsylvania, P.D.
WALTER ALLEN POWELL
Oil City, Pennsylvania, P.D.
CHARLES BEECHAM
Pennsylvania Game Commission
LANDON EUGENE WEAVER
Pennsylvania State Police
WALTER JOHN DEWITT III
Philadelphia, Pennsylvania, P.D.
ANTHONY JOHN NOTARO
Pittsburgh, Pennsylvania, P.D.
JAMES J MCVERRY
Pittsburgh, Pennsylvania, P.D.
JOHN DANDO
Shenandoah, Pennsylvania, C.O.
JOHN SIMON DERUBBO
Swissvale, Pennsylvania, P.D.
PETER J KROMER
Washington County, Pennsylvania, C.O.
ROBERT FLENNER
Waynesboro, Pennsylvania, P.D.
RALPH CLAIR HERROD
Westmont Borough, Pennsylvania, P.D.
CHARLES DAVIDSON
Westmoreland County, Pennsylvania, S.O.
GEORGE RIDGEWAY
Westmoreland County, Pennsylvania, S.O.

SOUTH CAROLINA
ROBERT HASELL
Berkeley County, South Carolina, C.O.
ALLEN LEE JACOBS
Greenville, South Carolina, P.D.
CHRISTIAN J D WOLFE
Orangeburg, South Carolina, Dept. of Public Safety
HOWARD H FRANKLIN
Orangeburg, South Carolina, Dept. of Public Safety
TENNESSEE
MARTIN TASE STURGILL II
Humphreys County, Tennessee, S.O.
ZACHARY TYLER LARNERD
Jackson County, Tennessee, S.O.
SEAN LEWIS ALLRED
Livingston, Tennesee, P.D.
KENNY RAY MOATS
Maryville, Tennessee, P.D.
VERDELL SMITH SR
Memphis, Tennessee, P.D.
JAMES JACKSON LEE
Putnam County, Tennessee, S.O.
ORVILLE AMOS MOSS
Putnam County, Tennessee, S.O.
DE'GREAUN RESHUN FRAZIER
Tennessee Bureau of Investigation
ROBERT TILMAN THOMASON
Washington County, Tennessee, S.O.
TEXAS
JUSTIN RYAN SCHERLEN
Amarillo, Texas, P.D.
AMIR ABDUL-KHALIQ
Austin, Texas, P.D.

MARCO ANTONIO ZARATE
Bellaire, Texas, P.D.
JAMES O LONG
Briscoe County, Texas, S.O.
MARION ABE BLEDSOE
Cleburne, Texas, P.D.
BRENT ALAN THOMPSON
Dallas Area Rapid Transit, Texas, P.D.
LORNE BRADLEY AHRENS
Dallas, Texas, P.D.
MICHAEL JOSEPH SMITH
Dallas, Texas, P.D.
MICHAEL LESLIE KROL
Dallas, Texas, P.D.
PATRICIO ENRIQUE ZAMARRIPA
Dallas, Texas, P.D.
KENNETH HUBERT MALTBY
Eastland County, Texas, S.O.
THAD DEWITT WEST
Ector County, Texas, S.O.
DAVID ORTIZ
El Paso, Texas, P.D.
DAVID STEFAN HOFER
Euless, Texas, P.D.
ROBERT E RANSOM
Gregg County, Texas, S.O.
STACEY ALLEN BAUMGARTNER
Patton Village, Texas, P.D.
ENDY NDDIOBONG EKPANYA
Pearland, Texas, P.D.
BENJAMIN MARCONI
San Antonio, Texas, P.D.
KENNETH JOSEPH STARRS
South Texas Specialized Crimes & Narcotics Task Force
CALVIN MARCUS MCCULLERS JR

Southern Methodist University, Texas, P.D.
MARI ANNE JOHNSON
Texas Department of Criminal Justice
JEFFREY DON NICHOLS
Texas Dept. of Public Safety
BEN PENNINGTON
Texas Rangers, Texas
ROBERT ERNEST HUNT
Texas Rangers, Texas
UTAH
LEON ALBERT MAY
Box Elder County, Utah. S.O.
DOUGLAS SCOTT BARNEY II
Unified P.D. of Greater Salt Lake, Utah
ERIC DALE ELLSWORTH
Utah Highway Patrol
CODY JAMES BROTHERSON
West Valley City, Utah, P.D.
VIRGINIA
HARVEY SNOOK III
Arlington County, Virginia, P.D.
ASHLEY MARIE GUINDON
Prince William County, Virginia, P.D.
CHAD PHILLIP DERMYER
Virginia State Police
WASHINGTON
GEORGE H YEAMAN JR
King County, Washington, S.O.
JOHN FREDERICK MINES
King County, Washington, S.O.
R JAKE GUTIERREZ
Tacoma, Washington, P.D.
WEST VIRGINIA
ROBERT LONG
Guyandotte, West Virginia, C.O.

ROY C KNOTTS
Logan, West Virginia, P.D.
EUGENE CRUM
Mingo County, West Virginia, S.O.
JOSEPH GEORGE PORTARO
West Virginia State Police
WISCONSIN
CHARLES WILLIAM GUDGELL
Milwaukee, Wisconsin, P.D.
ADAM JOHN HARTWIG
Ozaukee County, Wisconsin, S.O.
DAN THOMAS GLAZE JR
Rusk County, Wisconsin, S.O.
MICHAEL JOSUA VENTURA
Salem, Wisconsin, Dept. of Public Safety
FEDERAL AGENCIES
JERRY D JOBE
Federal Bureau of Investigation
PAUL H WILSON
Federal Bureau of Investigation
ROBERT MARTIN ROTH
Federal Bureau of Investigation
STEVEN A CARR
Federal Bureau of Investigation
WESLEY J YOO
Federal Bureau of Investigation

WILLIAM ROBERT CRAIG
Federal Bureau of Investigation
KCEY ELENA RUIZ
U.S. Air Force, Security Forces Directorate
NATHAN COLE SARTAIN
U.S. Air Force, Security Forces Directorate
JAMES DENNIS MCNAUGHTON
U.S. Army Reserve

DAVID GOMEZ
U.S. Border Patrol
JOSE DANIEL BARRAZA
U.S. Border Patrol
MANUEL ALEJANDRO ALVAREZ
U.S. Border Patrol
JAVIER VEGA JR
U.S. Border Patrol
BRIAN PECSON BELISO
U.S. Department of Homeland Security, ICE
J SCOTT MCGUIRE
U.S. Department of Homeland Security, ICE
PATRICK THOMAS CAROTHERS
U.S. Marshals Service
CHARLES GLEASON VENZ
U.S. Probation Office
JAMES STEVEN COLLINS
U.S. Secret Service
RAILROAD POLICE
THOMAS P GRIFFIN
Chicago, Rock Island & Pacific Railway, P.D.
STEVEN W HARTON
Denver and Rio Grande Railway, P.D.
JOHN L BEISSER
Pennsylvania Railroad, P.D.
LESTER E ROLAND
Southern Pacific Railroad, P.D.
MILFORD JAMES MERRIFIELD
Texas and Pacific Railroad, P.D.
LLOYD JAMES SPAUR
Union Pacific Railroad, P.D.
AMERICAN TERRITORIES
SIEGFRED D R MORTERA
Guam, P.D.

EDWIN R PABON-ROBLES
Puerto Rico, P.D.
LUIS A MELENDEZ-MALDONADO
Puerto Rico, P.D.
VICTOR M ROSADO-ROSA
Puerto Rico, P.D.
WALDEMAR RIVERA-SANTIAGO
Puerto Rico, P.D.

47
Police Glossary

A & B = Assault and Battery (Beat with Hands)
Abduction = To Take Forcefully
Affirmative = Yes
B&E = Breaking and entering (home or business)
B.O.L. = Be On the Lookout
Bought it = You have been killed
BSA = Blue Steel (Black Colored) Automatic Handgun
BSR = Blue Steel Revolver
Bull Pen = A large room-like holding cell with brick walls and stationary benches along the walls
Car = Accident Car = (Motor Car Example: 8M2
Car Jack = Steal a Vehicle with a Person Inside)
CCW = Carrying a Concealed Weapon
Chase = Police Pursuit of Motor Vehicle
C.O.S. = Communications Operations Section
DGH = Old Detroit General Hospital
D.O.A. = Dead on Arrival
D.O.S. = Dead on the Scene
D.W.I. = Driving While Intoxicated
F.A. = Felonious Assault (With Any Dangerous Weapon)
Fatal = Any Type of Death Other Than Natural
Felony = (A Serious Crime 2 or More Years in Prison)
Foot Chase = Chase Subject on Foot
44 Magnum = A 44 caliber gun with an extra load of gun powder, causing the bullet to achieve magnum force.
GDR = Golden Rule Drunk (Means No Crime Committed)
Home Invasion 1 = Break into Home with People Inside
Home Invasion 2 = Break into Home with No One Inside
I.A. = Internal Affairs

John Doe = A Person either Dead or Alive. No I.D.
Kidnap = To Take a Child Forcefully
Killing = A Homicide
L.E.I.N. = Law Enforcement Information Network
Long Gun = A Rifle or Shotgun
Misdemeanor = A Minor Crime 90 Days to 1 Year in Jail
M.O. = Method of Operation
Negative = No
N.C.I.C. = National Crime Information Center (for crime across the nation and in all 52 states)
NPA = Nickel Plated Automatic (Silver Color)
NPR = Nickel Plated Revolver
Officer in Trouble = Officer Needs Help Right Away. Life is in Danger
One Down = A Person Dead, Unconscious or Injured
ORD = Ordinance = (Traffic Ticket)
Perp = Perpetrator
Plate = License Plate Number
Platoon One = Midnight shift
Platoon Two = Day shift
Platoon Three – Afternoon shift
P.R.E.P. = (Personal Radio Equipped Patrolman)
Priority One = The Most Serious of Police Runs
RA = Robbery Armed (With any weapon)
RNA = Robbery Not Armed (Purse Snatch)
Roll Over = Car or Truck Over Turned
TSS = Tactical Services Section
30 Series = Plain Car = 15-30 Means 15th Prec 30 Series
U.D.A.A. = Unlawfully Drive Away Auto (Steal a Car)
V.I.N. = Vehicle Identification Number

ABOUT THE AUTHOR

Born and raised in Detroit, Lee Richardson's love for the Detroit Police Department and the community encouraged him to return to work after retirement. He is now serving as a Communications Instructor at the Wayne County Community College and teaching young millenniums now to be police dispatchers.

Contact Information:
Mr. Lee Richardson, Jr.
P.O. Box 231139
Detroit, MI 48223

Made in the USA
Monee, IL
04 November 2026

67386598R00105